Conquering Math Myths
with
Universal Design

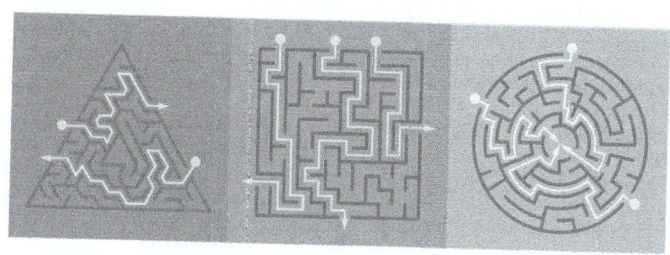

Conquering Math Myths with Universal Design

An Inclusive Instructional Approach for Grades K–8

JENNA MANCINI RUFO & RON MARTIELLO

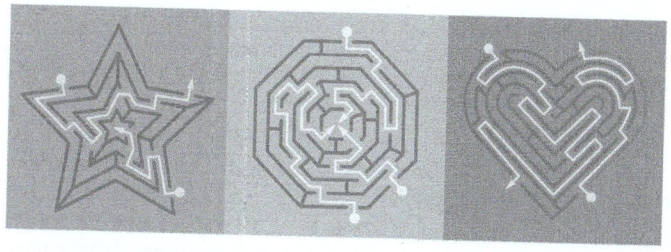

Arlington, Virginia USA

2800 Shirlington Road, Suite 1001 • Arlington, VA 22206 USA
Phone: 800-933-2723 or 703-578-9600 • Fax: 703-575-5400
Website: www.ascd.org • Email: member@ascd.org
Author guidelines: www.ascd.org/write

Richard Culatta, Chief Executive Officer; Anthony Rebora, *Chief Content Officer;* Genny Ostertag, *Managing Director, Book Acquisitions & Editing;* Stephanie Bize, *Acquisitions Editor;* Mary Beth Nielsen, *Director, Book Editing;* Jennifer L. Morgan, *Editor;* Lisa Hill, *Graphic Designer;* Cynthia Stock, *Typesetter;* Kelly Marshall, *Production Manager;* Shajuan Martin, *E-Publishing Specialist;* Kathryn Oliver, *Creative Project Manager*

Copyright © 2024 ASCD. All rights reserved. It is illegal to reproduce copies of this work in print or electronic format (including reproductions displayed on a secure intranet or stored in a retrieval system or other electronic storage device from which copies can be made or displayed) without the prior written permission of the publisher. By purchasing only authorized electronic or print editions and not participating in or encouraging piracy of copyrighted materials, you support the rights of authors and publishers. Readers who wish to reproduce or republish excerpts of this work in print or electronic format may do so for a small fee by contacting the Copyright Clearance Center (CCC), 222 Rosewood Dr., Danvers, MA 01923, USA (phone: 978-750-8400; fax: 978-646-8600; web: www.copyright.com). To inquire about site licensing options or any other reuse, contact ASCD Permissions at www.ascd.org/permissions or permissions@ascd.org. For a list of vendors authorized to license ASCD ebooks to institutions, see www.ascd.org/epubs. Send translation inquiries to translations@ascd.org.

ASCD® is a registered trademark of Association for Supervision and Curriculum Development. All other trademarks contained in this book are the property of, and reserved by, their respective owners, and are used for editorial and informational purposes only. No such use should be construed to imply sponsorship or endorsement of the book by the respective owners.

All web links in this book are correct as of the publication date below but may have become inactive or otherwise modified since that time. If you notice a deactivated or changed link, please email books@ascd.org with the words "Link Update" in the subject line. In your message, please specify the web link, the book title, and the page number on which the link appears.

PAPERBACK ISBN: 978-1-4166-3306-8 ASCD product #124004 n8/24
PDF EBOOK ISBN: 978-1-4166-3307-5; see Books in Print for other formats.
Quantity discounts are available: email programteam@ascd.org or call 800-933-2723, ext. 5773, or 703-575-5773. For desk copies, go to www.ascd.org/deskcopy.

Library of Congress Cataloging-in-Publication Data

Names: Rufo, Jenna M., author. | Martiello, Ron, author.
Title: Conquering math myths with universal design : an inclusive instructional approach for grades K–8 / Jenna Mancini Rufo and Ron Martiello.
Description: Arlington, Virginia : ASCD, [2024] | Includes bibliographical references and index.
Identifiers: LCCN 2024014858 (print) | LCCN 2024014859 (ebook) | ISBN 9781416633068 (paperback) | ISBN 9781416633075 (pdf)
Subjects: LCSH: Mathematics—Study and teaching (Elementary) | Inclusive education.
Classification: LCC QA135.6 .R84 2024 (print) | LCC QA135.6 (ebook) | DDC 372.7/044—dc23/eng/20240628
LC record available at https://lccn.loc.gov/2024014858
LC ebook record available at https://lccn.loc.gov/2024014859

33 32 31 30 29 28 27 26 25 24   1 2 3 4 5 6 7 8 9 10 11 12

Conquering Math Myths with Universal Design

Acknowledgments vii

1. The Haunting of Math by Myths 1
2. UDL as the Antidote to Math Myths 10
3. The Math Person Myth: Building Positive Math Identities 19
4. The Learning Gaps Myth: Planning with Focus and Coherence 32
5. The Answer Getting Myth: Developing Conceptual Understanding 45
6. The Rigor Myth: Designing Rigorous Learning Experiences for All 59
7. The Single Score Myth: Using Balanced Assessment to Guide Instruction 75
8. The All Children, but . . . Myth: Creating Systems of Equity and Excellence 88

References 100

Index 107

About the Authors 111

Acknowledgments

From Jenna

Oftentimes, the idea of writing a book conjures up an image of the tortured author struggling with writer's block or laboring for hours over a computer. Although there was a little bit of that, writing this book was mostly...*fun*! One of my fondest memories of the writing process was spending time with my daughter Emma. Emma sat on the floor of my office, drawing fractional parts and lending her penmanship for our graphics while I wrote. Thank you, Emma, for your contribution and for your beautiful soul.

I must express my heartfelt thanks to my husband, Patrick, for his unending support of me and for giving me the time and space to create. I love you and appreciate you. To my daughter Eva, who takes the world by storm—I appreciate your unique perspective and candor and can't wait to see what you grow up to be.

I must also thank my parents, Nick and Barb Mancini, and my sisters, Laura Belmont and Nina Mancini, for supporting me during a truly crazy year. And to my inclusionistas—Kate Small, Jackie Giammarco, Megan Klementisz, Kristy Johnson, Rachael Burg, and Aisha Weston—thank you for indulging all my crazy ideas about how to make the world a better, more inclusive place. You inspire me, and I'm so proud of the work we have achieved together.

Book number three has been my favorite yet, and that is largely due to my amazing co-author, Ron Martiello. Our partnership mirrored what collaboration in inclusive education should look like—two educators sharing ownership, building upon one another's strengths, and learning from each other along the way. I am so grateful to have shared this writing experience with Ron, who is not only a supportive colleague but also an amazing human.

From Ron

The work from this book does not happen without the love, care, and influence of others. In no way has my career path been a straight line. It started many years ago with the love and support of my mother, Pat Martiello, and my father, Ron Martiello Sr. I once told my father that I just wanted to be a teacher. He said, "No. You need to be the best teacher you can be." I worked for many years as a teacher and assistant principal to reach the position of principal, where I proudly served my school community for eight years. It was then that I made a heart-first decision to return to teaching and spend more time with my family. Thank you to my loving wife, Julie, and our children, Nick, Callie, and Nate, for their love and encouragement as I put down my principal hat and picked up my Little League coach's hat. It is that continued love and understanding that I take to work each day, inspired to make the world a little better place.

It is with great appreciation that I acknowledge my math colleagues and companions. Thank you for the times you provided feedback and moral support. Most importantly, thank you for our daily journey to support teachers and students in our district. Your commitment is unwavering.

Thank you to my co-author, Jenna Mancini Rufo. Writing can be a challenge for me. However, Jenna magically turned my rough drafts about mathematics and learning into something special. Jenna has been a trusted friend and colleague since my early days as a principal. I appreciate her genuine honesty, commitment to her cause, and unwavering dedication to family. Thank you again for writing this book with me.

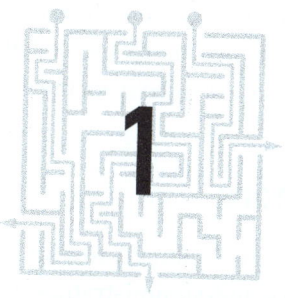

The Haunting of Math by Myths

The teaching and learning of mathematics have long been haunted by myths.

These myths permeate our schools, conjuring the illusion that math is an esoteric subject, only to be mastered by a select few. Math myths deceive teachers and students alike into adopting the narrow belief that mathematics is simply about answer getting—you're either right or you're wrong; you have the answer or you don't; you are a "math person" or you're not. Math myths fool us into thinking that test scores are the ultimate goal and that rigorous mathematics experiences are not for everyone. Math myths dupe us into thinking that students with "learning gaps" will never be successful in math, and that if we create inclusive mathematics classrooms, surely someone will suffer. Such mathematical folklore creates a false dichotomy in which equity and excellence are viewed as mutually exclusive.

We decided to write this book to bust the litany of math myths once and for all. In *Conquering Math Myths with Universal Design: An Inclusive Instructional Approach for Grades K–8*, we share how a universally designed approach to mathematics instruction is the antidote to widely accepted math fallacies. The Universal Design for Learning (UDL) framework provides students with multiple ways to access mathematical content, engage in authentic learning experiences, and share their knowledge. Such an approach creates classrooms where every student is equipped with the tools needed to succeed at high levels and where teachers and learners alike are freed from the shackles of math myths.

About the Authors

We, Jenna and Ron, have a combined 40-plus years of education experience as both teachers and administrators. We worked together for nearly 13 years in a large public school system where Jenna served as both an assistant superintendent and special education director, and Ron acted in the capacities of principal, instructional coach, and supervisor for mathematics.

Through our work together, we strived to create a system where all learners received quality experiences in general education classrooms, regardless of ability, language, or background. While a robust system of instruction and intervention was successful in supporting students in the area of literacy, we found achieving the same goal more challenging for mathematics. Why?

We intend to answer that question and more. However, before we do, let's pause and take a step back to examine the culture of teaching and learning mathematics. It isn't possible to shift such a culture until we understand why it exists. Mathematical classroom communities are shaped by individuals' "math stories"—many of which perpetuate math myths in education. We'll begin by sharing our own stories.

Jenna's Math Story: Just Not a "Math Person"

My first math memory dates back to 3rd grade. I can vividly recall the origins of my antipathy. As a shy, rule-following student, I was mortified when I found myself held back from recess one beautiful fall day because I had not finished my mathematics "seatwork"—independent workbook practice. If losing recess wasn't bad enough, the only other peer who remained in the classroom with me was Courtney—a classmate who, in my estimation, was clearly "not good at math." Courtney struggled to keep up with the rest of us in a classroom culture that had already established who the "math people" were by the ripe old age of 8. My embarrassment was overwhelming.

So strong was this feeling of humiliation that over 35 years later I still recall the activity that kept me from recess—counting sticks. The workbook required students to demonstrate knowledge of place value through counting illustrated bundles of sticks representing 1s, 10s, and 100s. As I hunched over my workbook with squinted eyes, tallying the sticks in each bundle, Courtney looked over at what I was doing and asked, "You know the small bundles are 10s and the big ones are 100s, right?" Did I know this? Of course not! Had I known I only needed to count by 10s or 100s, I would not have spent nearly 15 minutes of my valuable recess time counting minuscule individual sticks. With this newfound knowledge, I gleefully finished my seatwork, presented it to the teacher, and left Courtney behind (what a terrible friend I was). I then slinked off from the classroom to the playground in hopes that no one would remember why I was late.

I am confident that this experience had a lasting impact on my future relationship with math. I don't remember ever disliking math before the stick-counting experience. Afterward, however, I displayed a distinct reticence for the subject. I approached mathematical tasks with hesitancy and anxiety. Although I participated in advanced math coursework throughout my middle and high school years, I declined the opportunity to participate in an advanced placement calculus course for fear I couldn't hack it. *I just wasn't a math person.*

It wasn't until years later, when I found myself the sole instructor for an after-school mathematics intervention program for 6th through 8th graders, that I had an epiphany—*I actually AM a math person!* I enjoyed creating accessible math experiences for students who also believed that they just weren't math people. There was nothing better than working alongside students and observing the moment when math clicked for them. Today, I share my passion for mathematics and inclusion of students with diverse learning profiles through my work as an educational consultant.

Ron's Math Story: An On-Again/Off-Again Relationship

My love story with math began years ago, in Catholic grade school. I approached math with a confident swagger. You see, I was in contention to be the Knock Out champ each day. Not Basketball Knock Out—*Math* Knock Out. In this classroom game, everyone stood at their desks and, one at a time, recited answers to questions on math facts. Those who answered correctly remained standing, while those who answered incorrectly were demoted to watching the remainder of the game from the sidelines. The last one standing in Math Knock Out was deemed the champ of the day and received a sticker of their choice. My blue clip-on tie was adorned with many stickers of various cartoon characters, signifying my numerous victories. When stickers fell off my tie, I would find Mom's tape and reattach them.

My dynasty continued until the fall of 5th grade. At this point, some of my classmates were rostered into higher-level mathematics classes. I remained in the on-level class, where math was not as exciting. Here, the myth of rigor being appropriate only for some students prevailed—I was relegated to mathematical drills and mindless completion of algorithms. My love affair with math slowly fizzled until nothing was left. I felt indifferent. Math and I grew apart.

Fast-forward to high school, where I continued my lukewarm relationship with math in the "second track"—the track between the AP/honors classes and the "basic math" students. Unbeknownst to me at the time, the second track set lower expectations for my math future, leading to trigonometry but not calculus. Yet, despite my ambivalence, I earned *A*s in my math courses. I completed my work, compliant but not engaged, and my teachers were content with my mediocrity.

When I arrived at college, however, math blindsided me. My entrance exam results placed me in remedial algebra! I was confused. Apparently, math was "out of my league." This time, I decided to break up with math once and for all—I would complete my requirements and banish math from my life.

The breakup lasted 20 years, until I found myself in the position of having to teach math. Attending a professional development session revealed to me that I had bought into the myth that math was about answer getting. I shifted to more student-centered instruction, teaching multiple strategies and the use of tools to allow students to explore mathematical patterns and relationships. My love of math was rekindled, and my students began to experience a newfound appreciation of math. Math was fun, exciting, and better than ever. Today, math and I are happy together, and I share my love of math as an instructional coach.

Everyone Has a Math Story

Take a few minutes to reflect upon your math story. Did a traumatic math experience shape your attitude toward the topic, like Jenna? Or do you have an "on-again, off-again" relationship with math, affected by placement tests and tracked learning classes, like Ron? Have you bought into the idea that you aren't a "math person," or did you excel at math because you believe you are? Now think about your students who struggle with math. What do they believe about the subject? What are their math stories?

It is time to rewrite the math myths our students have long been told. In contrast with what is taught about other subjects, students have been indoctrinated to believe that math talent is an innate skill that is difficult to learn if they do not already possess that gift. Although we rarely hear "I'm just not a *reading* person" or "I'm just not a *writing* person," the choruses of "I am just not a *math* person" persist.

In *Conquering Math Myths with UDL*, we share how to develop a new, collective math story to dispel widely held math myths. Each chapter begins by focusing on a specific myth and related fallacies that negatively affect students. Next, we offer strategies and concrete examples of how you can use a UDL approach to bust the myth. The UDL framework facilitates the creation of accessible environments for all learners through multiple means of representation, engagement, and action and expression (CAST, 2018b). We explain how UDL and pillars of mathematics instruction intersect in clear and understandable terms to help you as you translate theory to practice. Here is a sneak preview of what's to come.

Chapter 2: UDL as the Antidote to Math Myths

Chapter 2 answers the essential question *How can we organize teaching and learning to address a wide range of learning profiles in the mathematics classroom?* We share how the inclusive UDL framework proactively and strategically accounts for learner variability through intentional design and reduction of predictable barriers. We explain how UDL principles provide a variety of access points to students and how these tenets are compatible with the pillars of mathematics. This chapter sets the stage for you to support students in reaching their highest potential and disproving entrenched math myths.

Chapter 3: The Math Person Myth: Building Positive Math Identities

The pervasive beliefs that mathematical ability is innate and that some individuals simply aren't "math people" are a widely accepted societal norm. Chapter 3 poses the essential question *How do we create classrooms where students and teachers embrace risk taking and build confidence in their math identity and ability?* Busting the myth of the math person is no small task. We offer strategies for actively engaging students in building positive math identities and partnering with them to create goals. We also share techniques to support student agency and specific ways to analyze mistakes. Finally, we address teachers who feel they are "math impostors" and support them in building their self-efficacy in math.

Chapter 4: The Learning Gaps Myth: Planning with Focus and Coherence

The myth of learning gaps is the belief that it is simply not possible to address all elements of the math curriculum without moving too quickly for some students and too slowly for others. This myth can result in two opposing approaches to math instruction. Some teachers, believing that all standards are created equally, race through the content, sacrificing depth for breadth. Others may insist that students master "prerequisite skills" before advancing to more challenging content. Both methods are problematic. Chapter 4 responds to the essential question *How can educators manage to fully address the mathematics curriculum while attending to differences in students' prior knowledge?* We illustrate how educators can plan with focus and coherence to both address learning gaps and extend activities. We share how to clarify goals, plan effective minilessons, and create tasks with "low floors and high ceilings."

Chapter 5: The Answer Getting Myth: Developing Conceptual Understanding

Chapter 5 challenges you to redefine success in mathematics. We reject the myth that math is simply about answer getting. Instead, shift your focus to honing precision and accuracy as ongoing processes rather than an endpoint. We share how to implement the Standards for Mathematical Practice (SMPs) in inclusive ways, facilitating flexible thinking and reasoning in students through the strategic use of tools and strategies. We present ways to organize opportunities for the exploration of structures, patterns, and relationships so that students become expert learners who can develop effective arguments. Finally, we offer suggestions on how to support students to persevere when presented with challenging tasks, addressing the essential question *How do we develop conceptual understanding in a way that promotes productive struggle without relying on tips and tricks?*

Chapter 6: The Rigor Myth: Designing Rigorous Learning Experiences for All

The myth of rigor assumes that a rigorous math classroom can only be implemented through overly challenging work. Some educators believe that only a select group of students are capable of achieving at high levels, and that students with learning challenges must be sheltered from rigorous instruction. Chapter 6 busts this myth by answering the essential question *How do we provide all students with access to rigorous learning tasks while supporting them in the learning process?* Rigor is not about making a task really hard for students, nor is it about privileging a select few while shielding others from unrealistic expectations. This chapter provides specific strategies to embrace the understanding that rigor in mathematics is for *all* students. We share how to achieve rigor in mathematic instruction with attention to conceptual understanding, procedural fluency, and real-world application.

Chapter 7: The Single Score Myth: Using Balanced Assessment to Guide Instruction

Chapter 7 poses the essential question *How do we implement a balanced approach where assessment is part of an ongoing process rather than a single event?* The myth that a single score defines students by end-of-unit or end-of-year test scores is pervasive in our schools. We encourage you to move away from physical or metaphorical "gold stars" and incorporate multiple forms of assessment to analyze student progress. This approach provides more nuanced information on student learning and accounts for both processes and solutions. We share multiple formative and summative assessment techniques to direct future instruction and learning, and close the chapter by encouraging educators to "assess with a heart" and embrace practices that allow for student mastery and go beyond simple grade assignment.

Chapter 8: The All Children, but . . . Myth: Creating Systems of Equity and Excellence

Chapter 8 is a call to action. This chapter grapples with the essential question *How can we create systems that promote both equity and excellence in mathematics so that "all" really means all?* Is striving toward a growth mindset an empty mantra in your district, or are systems designed to support students in growing? Are students assigned packets of activities, or do they have meaningful access to a viable and coherent curriculum? Do intervention and enrichment efforts contribute to widening the gaps in the educational system or do they coherently align to core instruction? Will your school system continue to separate students into special education classrooms for math, or will they commit to desegregating learning environments empowered by UDL? The pursuit of equity and excellence can only be achieved through a systematic approach fueled by collective courage. We cannot do this alone. This chapter provides the research and the guidance for your organization to develop a system where all truly means all.

An Invitation

Now we offer you an invitation to abandon the math myths you have been programmed to believe. Instead, write a new math story. This tale will be bold and fierce in its approach. It will dismiss the belief that math is for a chosen few in favor of the courageous philosophy that math is for *all*!

Our story is not a fairy tale.

Instead of castles, there are classrooms—classrooms where students are engaged and believe in themselves.

Instead of knights and princesses, there are heroes—teachers who inspire students to take risks and boldly solve problems.

Instead of a happily ever after ending, there is the understanding that learning is not that linear, and success is found in the journey.

Won't you come along for the ride?

UDL as the Antidote to Math Myths

How can we organize teaching and learning to address a wide range of learning profiles in the mathematics classroom?

Many of today's pervasive math myths are perpetuated by a teaching approach grounded in the traditional methodology of whole-group instruction. Mathematical content presented in just one, narrow way to the whole class leads to struggle for learners who cannot grasp the content in that particular way. A one-size-fits-all approach to learning will never allow each learner to realize their full potential because offering students "the same instruction on the same content standards in the same general education classrooms ... offers the same historic results—large and persistent gaps in achievement" (Elliott et al., 2014, p. 4). How, then, can we organize teaching and learning to address a wide range of learning preferences in the mathematics classroom?

Enter UDL: Universal Design for Learning.

The concept of universal design originated in the field of architecture. Architect Ronald Mace, who had contracted polio at a young age, became frustrated at his inability to access buildings in his wheelchair. He began advocating for the use of "a design that's usable by all people, to the greatest extent possible, without the need for adaptation or specialized design" (Mace, 1985, as cited in Pruett, 2017).

Rather than retrofitting buildings with ramps, power doors, and accessible bathrooms, Mace proposed that buildings be designed inclusively from the start. As Mace's ideas took root and the principles of universal design were implemented in architecture, people realized that designs that were necessary for people with disabilities were beneficial to everyone. For example, a curb cut is essential for a wheelchair user but also helpful to someone pushing a baby stroller or shopping cart. Automatic doors are necessary for an individual with a physical impairment but also useful for someone carrying a box.

Similarly, Universal Design for Learning recognizes that designing instruction with everyone in mind from the start creates better learning experiences for all students, not just those with learning challenges. UDL is often defined as a brain-based framework for instructional design that provides students with multiple means of representation, engagement, and action and expression (CAST, n.d.). But what exactly does that mean? Let's break UDL down into its key components. The UDL framework does the following:

- Targets inclusive instruction
- Accounts for individual variability
- Is intentionally designed
- Reduces predictable barriers to learning
- Provides multiple ways for students to access information, express their knowledge, and engage with the content

In this chapter, we will further explore each component to help you apply these elements of UDL to the daily mathematical practice in your classroom.

UDL as a Framework for Inclusive Instruction

The education system has a long history of segregating students. *Brown v. Board of Education* (1954) ruled that separate is "inherently unequal" and that designating separate schools for students based on race is unconstitutional. *Lau v. Nichols* (1974) prohibited discrimination against students on the basis of national origin, finding that schools must provide language instruction for non-English speaking students. The Individuals with Disabilities Education Improvement Act (IDEIA, 2004), the federal special education law, has long been anchored in the tenet of "least restrictive environment," setting a standard that students with disabilities must be educated with their nondisabled peers in general education classrooms to the maximum extent appropriate. Time and time again, courts have ruled that educational segregation is illegal.

Yet despite these laws, historically marginalized groups continue to be relegated to separate instruction and to experience persistent negative outcomes. Black, Hispanic, and Indigenous students are underrepresented in higher-level coursework (Mullaguru, 2016). Students with disabilities and English language learners (ELLs) continue to experience the worst outcomes on the National Assessment of Educational Progress (NAEP) (The Nation's Report Card, 2022).

The UDL framework can assist educators in organizing their instruction to meet a wide range of student strengths and needs in the classroom. Inclusive education is the philosophy that all students deserve equal access and opportunity; UDL provides the structure to implement that philosophy, abandoning the idea that students must be separated and grouped according to perceived ability or characteristics. UDL offers a proactive, rather than reactive, approach to lesson design. Instead of creating a lesson and then layering on accommodations and modifications, educators design inclusive lessons from the start (Bartlett & Ehrlich, 2020). Teachers implementing UDL acknowledge that no two learners are alike, and they expect and plan for these differences.

Embracing Student Variability

Consider the labels commonly assigned to students in schools. A student who has a disability is an "IEP (individualized education plan) kid" or "special education student." One who speaks another language is an "ELL." Economically disadvantaged students are "Title I kids." The "really smart" children are deemed "gifted and talented." These labels shape both teacher perceptions of student abilities and the ways students view themselves. Math is especially susceptible to this type of labeling, due to the widespread—but misguided—belief that math is an innate talent.

We refer to instructional practices that separate students based on perceived characteristics as "labeling and sorting." After students are labeled, either through formal or informal assessment processes, the sorting begins. Students are clustered by ability into groups within the classroom. Nonproficient math students may be sent out of the room to receive support from an interventionist or specialist. These actions may be well-intentioned, but such practices reduce learning expectations for students and perpetuate the learning gaps we are trying so hard to close. Removing students with diverse learning needs from the classroom allows us to continue to deliver math instruction in a way that is not accessible to all students, reinforcing an exclusionary system.

Instead of viewing student differences as weaknesses that must be remediated through separation, UDL embraces the principle of learner variability. Variability can be thought of as all the unique strengths and weaknesses that make up an individual's learning profile (Jackson et al., 2020). Variability is ever-present in today's mathematics classrooms. It is found in the student with a learning disability who struggles with completing word problems but is skilled at creating visual models. It is evident in the high-achieving student who excels in solving challenging mathematical tasks but has difficulty explaining the reasoning behind the solutions. Variability is present in the student who appears distracted and unfocused during whole-group instruction but is highly engaged when working with peers.

These patterns of learning assets and challenges are dynamic and ever-changing due to the brain's ability to learn and adapt (Chardin &

Novak, 2021). Each individual has areas in which they excel and others in which they struggle. When this concept is considered within the context of a classroom containing several dozen students, we realize that there are endless strengths and needs in a single room.

Yet if it is widely accepted that no two individuals are the same, why do we continue to teach all of our students in the same way? Rather than planning narrow instruction targeted toward the mythical "average" student, teachers using UDL operate with the expectation of variability and intentionally plan accordingly. Learner variability should inform instructional design (Pape, 2018).

Deliberate and Intentional Lesson Design

Any teacher who has implemented multiple IEPs at once knows that determining how to deliver so many accommodations and modifications can feel unwieldy. It can be challenging to keep track of who gets extended time, who tests in a small group, who needs a completely different version of a worksheet, and so on. UDL takes a different approach.

Instead of adding accommodations and modifications after the fact, educators using a UDL framework proactively plan by considering a wide range of student strengths, needs, and preferences to create accessible lessons. UDL does not mean developing multiple lesson plans and goals for a single activity, nor does it mean retrofitting an already developed lesson to comply with students' IEPs. Let's take a closer look at how to apply UDL to math instruction in the classroom.

To intentionally design instruction with variability in mind, start with the goal. The goal of a lesson describes what a student should be able to know and do after instruction. Notice that we did not say that the goal should specify *how* an activity is completed. When developing goals, it is important to separate the *how* from the *what*. UDL provides multiple options for the *how* of learning for wider accessibility. Goals that are too narrow create unintentional barriers for students. Following is an example of how a narrowly crafted goal could be changed to account for learner variability.

> Mr. Wright is teaching his 4th grade students about equivalent fractions. The goal of his lesson is stated as follows: *Students will*

multiply a fraction's numerator and denominator by the same number to find equivalent fractions. Mr. Wright shows his students how to find an equivalent fraction for ⅓ by writing the following example on the board:

$$\frac{1}{3} \times \frac{2}{2} = \frac{2}{6}$$

He then shares several similar examples and provides students with a worksheet for independent practice.

In this example, Mr. Wright provided an algorithm to his students to teach them how to find equivalent fractions. It's a common way to introduce the concept, but it highlights a couple of problems. First, students learn the algorithm in isolation, without understanding what it truly represents. Second, there are multiple ways students could demonstrate their knowledge of equivalent fractions besides using a formula. By adjusting the goal to account for learner variability, Mr. Wright could engage a wider range of students in his class. To incorporate the principles of UDL into his goal, Mr. Wright could edit the learning outcome to say: *Students will use preferred tools and strategies to find equivalent fractions.*

This new goal, which does not specify the *how* of finding equivalent fractions, allows students to use a variety of approaches to demonstrate their knowledge. Some students might use fraction tiles to create equivalent fractions. Other students might create a drawing. And still others might use an algorithm to show understanding of the concept. (See Figures 2.1, 2.2, and 2.3 for illustrations of these approaches.)

Figure 2.1 Equivalent Fractions Using Fraction Tiles

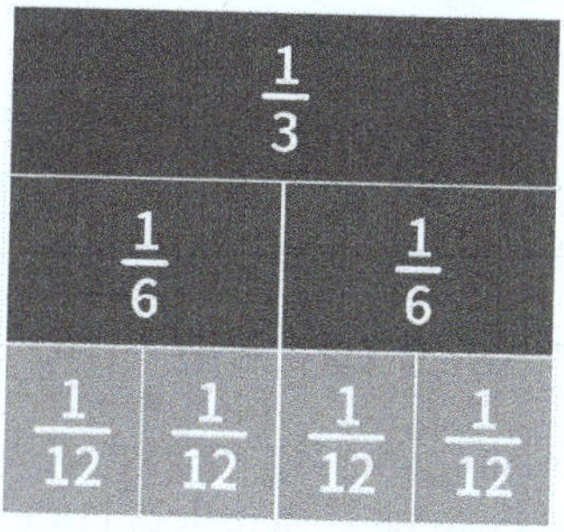

Figure 2.2 Equivalent Fractions Using Drawing

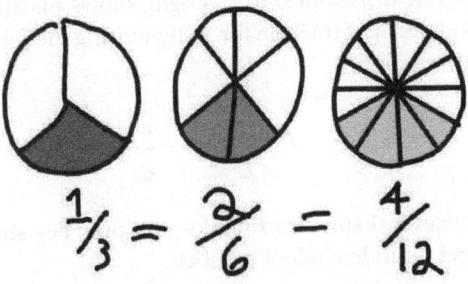

$$\frac{1}{3} = \frac{2}{6} = \frac{4}{12}$$

Figure 2.3 Equivalent Fractions Using Algorithm

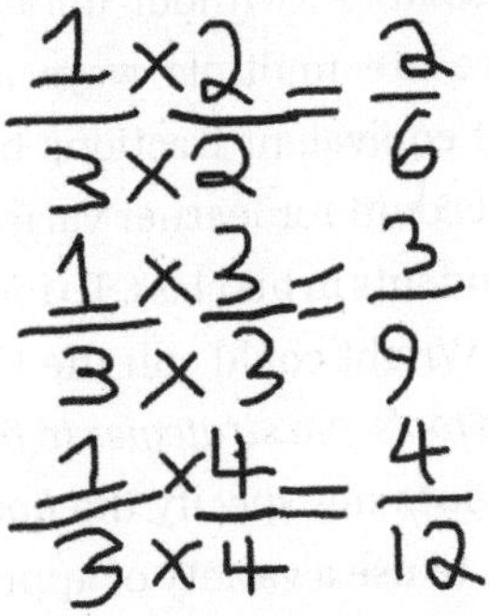

$$\frac{1 \times 2}{3 \times 2} = \frac{2}{6}$$

$$\frac{1 \times 3}{3 \times 3} = \frac{3}{9}$$

$$\frac{1 \times 4}{3 \times 4} = \frac{4}{12}$$

Broadening the learning goal to focus on the skill rather than the method of completion allows more students to access the lesson. This idea has been referred to as "tight goals, flexible means" (Bacon, 2014, para. 2). When educators intentionally tighten the goal, they clarify the learning outcomes and expectations for students. Flexibility with the means of completion communicates that there are multiple ways to achieve the goal. This recognition provides students the autonomy to approach tasks in ways that are most meaningful to them.

Reducing Barriers to Learning

In nearly every facet of life, you will find barriers to achieving your goals. Many of these barriers can be anticipated. For example, if you embark on a road trip in the middle of rush hour, you can expect to encounter traffic. Going to the grocery store with a small child often results in requests for unnecessary snacks or candy. Very few people go to the Department of Motor Vehicles (DMV) anticipating a quick and easy transaction. In these examples, the barriers are generally foreseeable and can be planned for—you can leave after rush hour, avoid the candy aisle, or clear your calendar on the day you need to go to the DMV—to achieve a better outcome.

Teaching is similar in that predictable learning barriers can often be expected and planned for. A key principle of UDL is anticipating these barriers and actively mitigating them by creating multiple pathways for students to reach a goal. Some students gain knowledge better through auditory means than visual representations. Children acquiring a second language may need picture supports to access learning. Individuals with sensory disabilities such as visual and hearing impairments will need a method of representation that removes barriers related to their disabilities. No single presentation method will be effective for all learners; therefore, it is essential to provide multiple ways for students to access material.

For example, students with reading disabilities may struggle to realize their math potential when presented with the barrier of language-based mathematical problems. Digital text-to-speech options, choral readings of the problems, pictorial supports, and opportunities to review and clarify vocabulary are all helpful strategies to work around language barriers. Lack of fluency and automaticity with math facts also present barriers. While students work toward mastery of facts, tools like calculators, number lines, and fact charts can support students in conceptual understanding of the task at hand. Predictable barriers unrelated to mathematical content may include math lessons scheduled during a challenging part of the day, such as first thing in the morning for tired teenagers or immediately after recess for kindergartners. In these instances, incorporating movement into lessons may be necessary for the morning crew, while a "settle down" routine might be useful for the rowdy post-recess bunch. The key to addressing all of these examples is identifying the barrier and planning around it so students can access the content, engage with the lesson, and respond meaningfully.

Choice and variety in response methods go hand-in-hand with student engagement. An overreliance on one form of output can be problematic for students who excel using a different method. When students have greater flexibility in choosing the method to demonstrate their knowledge, they will take greater ownership of their learning. Providing authentic contexts for learning and a rationale as to why the content is important is helpful in reducing the frequent choruses of "But how will I ever use this in real life?"—a predictable engagement barrier with upper elementary and secondary school students.

When designing lessons, consider barriers related to both instruction and the environment. Then, actively identify a strategy that could be implemented to reduce or eliminate the barrier. Finally, make that strategy available to all students whenever possible. Following this process will help you account for student variability and provide multiple ways for students to demonstrate their knowledge, access information, and engage with content (Posey, n.d.).

In the chapters that follow, we will provide you with concrete examples of how to use UDL in your mathematics classroom to debunk prevalent math myths and misconceptions.

Summary

Educators implementing a UDL approach to math clearly identify the *what* (the goal) of learning while providing choice and flexibility in *how* students reach and demonstrate that goal. They present students with lesson content in a variety of ways to account for individual variability rather than using a one-size-fits-all model. Teachers thoughtfully and intentionally plan lessons by considering predictable learning and engagement barriers in advance and explicitly designing ways to mitigate them. Students take ownership of their learning through choice and engagement with varied activities.

3

The Math Person Myth: Building Positive Math Identities

How do we create classrooms where students and teachers embrace risk taking and build confidence in their math identities and abilities?

Perhaps one of the most prevalent math myths is the myth that you're either a "math person"—or you're not. This widely held fallacy implies that mathematical aptitude is innate and difficult to develop. You either "have it" or you don't. But this is simply untrue. Math is for everyone—and when we say "everyone," we mean *everyone*.

To conquer the Math Person Myth, we need to understand the concept of "math identity." Students' math identities are shaped by their prior experiences with math (Anderson, 2007). These include the types of instruction they've received, their perceived success or lack of success with math, and their relationships with teachers and peers in math classrooms. Math identity comprises the attitudes and beliefs students hold about their abilities to perform successfully in mathematical contexts, both in and out of school (Aguirre et al., 2013).

The idea that such belief systems can have a significant impact on student performance raises questions such as the following:

- How much potential has gone undetected and underdeveloped from one generation of learners to the next as a result of emotional baggage related to math?
- How many students have been indoctrinated with the false belief that math proficiency is only attainable by a chosen few?
- How many children view math as a subject to endure rather than enjoy?

In this chapter, we will review how to develop positive math identities in students through shared goal setting, student agency, and intentional instructional strategies. We will also discuss the critical importance of both student and teacher self-efficacy in mathematics to eradicate the widespread Math Person Myth.

Offshoots of the Math Person Myth

The Bluebirds and Red Robins Myth

Schools operate as systems largely built on labeling and sorting (Rufo & Causton, 2022). At an early age, students are typically placed into ability groups for math and reading instruction, often disguised with cute names like "the bluebirds" and "the red robins," or "the green team" and "the yellow team." Ability grouping has gained increasing popularity in recent years, but evidence on its effectiveness is inconclusive (Bolick & Rogowsky, 2016). Due to the potential for ability grouping to widen skill gaps between students and create negative beliefs about perceived ability, teachers must proceed with extreme caution when considering the practice. Although such grouping may result in easier instructional management for teachers, we have observed that students placed in low groups quickly realize which group is the "smart" group and whether or not they are part of that elite faction. They then internalize those beliefs, leading to assumption of the "not a math person" identity—the very myth we are striving to conquer.

The Struggler Myth

Students who are relegated to lower math groups or separate programs earn the label of "struggler." Whether referred to as low achievers, at-risk, or even "fragile learners" (as if they might break), students trapped by this myth perceive limits on any future hope for math achievement, beset by insurmountable obstacles, blame, and complacency. Students with low math achievement may have their instruction outsourced to a specialist or special education teacher to "give them what they need." But this hollow promise can lead to students either lacking access to grade-level curricula or being oversupported and kept from opportunities to attempt challenging tasks. After all, strugglers are not "math people," so educators assume they require more assistance and support. Such an approach cheats students of fully realizing their math potential because it prevents them from receiving the types of exposure and challenge that are necessary for higher-level learning.

The Math Impostor Myth

The Math Person Myth is so deeply ingrained in our society that even some math teachers believe they are not math people! We call this "math impostor syndrome," and it is most frequently found in elementary math teachers who are generalists rather than specialists in the subject. Teachers caught up in this myth lack confidence in their own abilities. They "stick to the script," paging through the textbook and keeping the teacher's guide at the ready. They may be reluctant to provide students with greater choice and autonomy because they feel uncertain about math themselves. Because teachers' self-efficacy in instruction and classroom management has been found to affect students' attitudes about mathematics (Küçükalioğlu & Tuluk, 2021), teachers must address their own emotional baggage related to math to avoid creating another generation of self-proclaimed math impostors.

Fortunately, we can rewrite the narrative circling around the Math Person Myth by intentionally working to develop positive mathematical identities in students and improve self-efficacy in mathematics in teachers. It involves building a classroom community where goal setting, student agency, and universally designed tasks are prioritized. Students and teachers in these types of mathematical communities view mistakes as opportunities for growth and reject the idea that there is such a thing as a "math person."

Building Positive Math Identities

Students with positive academic mindsets have been found to put forth more effort in their work, productively engage in academic behaviors, and persevere when presented with difficult tasks (Farrington, 2013). However, many students approach mathematics with apprehension, viewing it as a system of rules to be followed and formulas to apply (Allen & Schnell, 2016). Student attitudes toward mathematics result from their previous mathematical experiences with content, teachers, and peers (Anderson, 2007). The emotions and preconceptions students bring to the math classroom present an additional hurdle, particularly for math teachers in the upper grades.

Perceptions are powerful. They can motivate learners to exceed expectations or stop them from ever engaging. To understand the beliefs students hold about their abilities in mathematics, teachers must proactively seek out information about their perceptions. Have students reflect on their math experiences through tools such as surveys, choice boards, interest inventories, interviews, and conferences. These activities can be used as baseline measures at the start of the school year and progress indicators throughout the year. Such tools can provide a valuable window into the positive or negative views students hold about both math and their own abilities.

Once students have shared their feelings about math, take time to debunk any math myths that arise (many of which you'll encounter in this and later chapters). Explicitly state to students that mathematics ability is not a fixed attribute—a tenet backed by brain research showing that the brain is incredibly flexible and constantly changing (Voss et al., 2017). You can then work alongside students to create goals and solutions to overcome those perceptual barriers. No effort is too small when it comes to making sure students feel like they belong in your math learning community.

A math mindset choice board like the one depicted in Figure 3.1 is an example of using UDL to gain insight into students' perceptions about math.

Figure 3.1 UDL Toolbox: Reflecting on Mindset

Strategy: Math Mindset Choice Board

Consider the following questions as you reflect on your feelings about math:
- What do you like about math?
- What do you dislike?
- How do you feel about the subject?
- What are your hopes for math this year?

Choose a way to share your reflections from the options below.

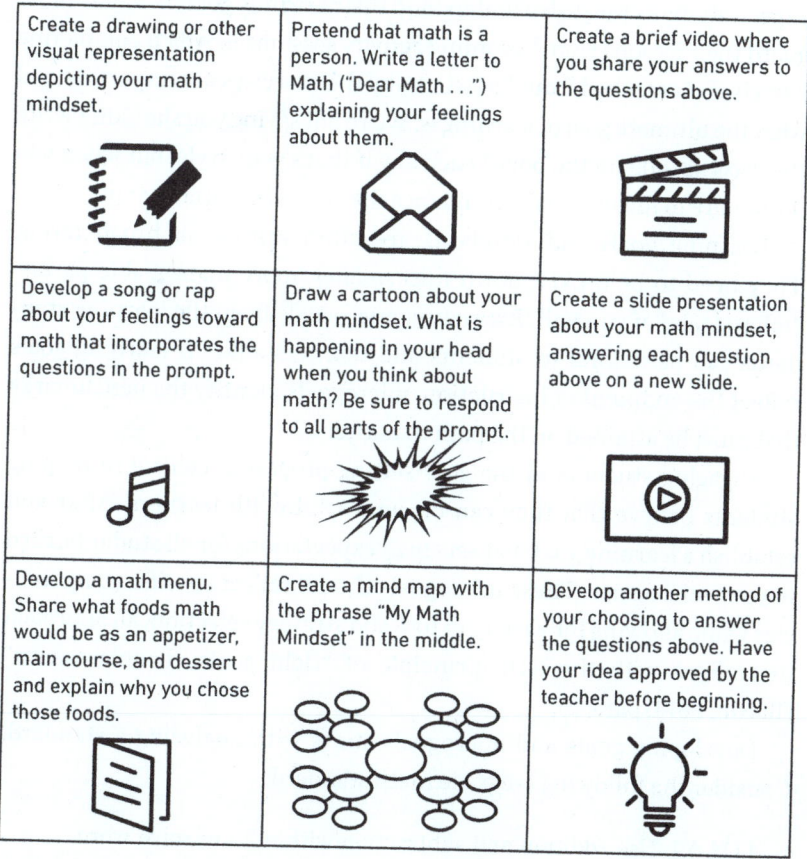

Create a drawing or other visual representation depicting your math mindset.	Pretend that math is a person. Write a letter to Math ("Dear Math . . .") explaining your feelings about them.	Create a brief video where you share your answers to the questions above.
Develop a song or rap about your feelings toward math that incorporates the questions in the prompt.	Draw a cartoon about your math mindset. What is happening in your head when you think about math? Be sure to respond to all parts of the prompt.	Create a slide presentation about your math mindset, answering each question above on a new slide.
Develop a math menu. Share what foods math would be as an appetizer, main course, and dessert and explain why you chose those foods.	Create a mind map with the phrase "My Math Mindset" in the middle.	Develop another method of your choosing to answer the questions above. Have your idea approved by the teacher before beginning.

Setting Goals and Microgoals

Renowned baseball player and coach Yogi Berra once said, "If you don't know where you're going, you might not get there." Partnering with students to set goals is a way to apply Yogi's wisdom to the math classroom by supporting students in understanding both where they're going and how they will arrive at the destination. Students will become more capable math learners when they understand the overarching goals of a lesson and develop personalized goals for themselves. This requires going a step beyond simply writing a lesson objective on the board.

It is important to recognize the difference between goals and agendas. Goals state learning outcomes, whereas agendas list activities to complete. Although agendas can be very helpful in informing students of what to expect, students must also understand their learning goal. Teachers must guard their lessons from becoming activity sessions in which completing exercises is detached from knowing why the exercises are important and what the ultimate goal of learning is. We're not saying you shouldn't write the class agenda on the board each day if that's your style, but when you do, be sure to include goals to enhance the class's comprehension.

Learning goals and standards are often worded in broad terms. They need to be broken down into smaller, more manageable parts—"microgoals," if you will. Extracting microgoals from the learning standards can be helpful to students and teachers alike. If learning goals reflect the endpoint of instruction, microgoals identify the benchmarks that must be attained on the path to mastery.

Engaging students in the goal-setting process is central in helping students believe that they can be successful math learners. After you establish a learning goal that sets high expectations for all students, turn to your microgoals. These microgoals should reflect specific competencies while allowing for variety in tool and strategy selection, an approach that aligns with the UDL principle of "tight goals, flexible means" (Bacon, 2014, para. 2).

Developing goals and microgoals starts with analyzing a standard. Consider the following 1st grade math standard:

> 1.OA.A.1. Use addition and subtraction within 20 to solve word problems involving situations of adding to, taking from, putting

together, taking apart, and comparing, with unknowns in all positions, e.g., by using objects, drawings, and equations with a symbol for the unknown number to represent the problem. (National Governors Association Center for Best Practices, Council of Chief State School Officers [CCSSO], 2010, p. 15)

This standard contains a multitude of learning objectives and needs to be scaffolded. There is no way that 6-year-olds could learn everything stated here in a single lesson, nor could their teacher instruct it all in a single class. Yet we must also guard ourselves from overgeneralizing by using catchall terms like problem solving. Adding to, taking from, putting together, taking apart, and comparing are components that help students make sense of addition and subtraction problems. Each component can be crafted into intentional learning objectives.

The multiple objectives within the standard that students will need to grasp to attain mastery are your microgoals. To develop a mathematics community where students are active participants in their learning—a necessity in developing healthy math identities—frame the microgoals as "I can" statements. Microgoals for the standard above could include the following:

- I can solve word problems that involve putting items together.
- I can take items apart to solve subtraction problems.
- I can use what I know about addition and subtraction to solve problems.
- I can find the unknown start number, change number, or end number.
- I know when I need to add or subtract when solving a comparison problem.

Providing clarity, allowing students to codesign learning intentions and microgoals, and developing a clear but flexible path to achievement are all methods to support students in embracing positive math identities.

Developing Student Agency

Student agency is the active involvement and empowerment of students to direct their learning (O'Rourke & Addison, 2017). Fostering student agency involves moving from traditional, teacher-led instruction to a greater focus on student-centered learning (Ferlazzo, 2019). Teachers can engender student agency by providing their students with grade-level-appropriate tasks to perform with the skills and strategies they have already acquired, which in turn promotes positive math identities as students successfully apply their knowledge.

You can support student agency by supplying your students with a wide range of physical tools and visual supports. These may include physical objects, displays, or posted reminders of previously taught strategies and procedures. Tools like these help students make sense of problems and look for entry points for solution attempts without relying on teacher intervention.

Providing students with multiple tools for construction and composition is an important feature of UDL. According to CAST (2018a),

> Unless a lesson is focused on learning to use a specific tool (e.g., learning to draw with a compass), curricula should allow many alternatives. Like any craftsman, learners should learn to use tools that are an optimal match between their abilities and the demands of the task. (para. 1)

Even very young students can be empowered to select the mathematical tools most meaningful to them. Take, for example, Ms. MacLuckie and Ms. Thamm's co-taught inclusive kindergarten class, made up of students with diverse learning profiles. After Ms. MacLuckie and Ms. Thamm provided instruction on the concept of length and measurement, students self-selected stations to practice their learning. Station 1 presented students with the opportunity to build structures with connecting cubes and measure them. Station 2 allowed students to use play dough to create and measure objects of various lengths. Station 3 required students to cut out pictures of flowers and measure their stems.

As students engaged with the stations, the teachers circulated the room with clipboards, recording student performance data using single-point rubrics to authentically assess student knowledge. Ms. MacLuckie and Ms. Thamm recognized that students can become expert learners when they are able to choose the tools and strategies that are most meaningful to them. Additionally, these co-teachers understood that there are more ways to evaluate student progress than just paper-and-pencil tasks.

A classroom that supports student agency is one in which students collaborate with one another about their choices and can articulate why they went about solving a problem in a certain way. Learners begin to evaluate their own reasoning and strategies to solve different problems. But this level of agency takes students beyond simply engaging in daily problem solving.

Treating Mistakes as Opportunities

As students become more active participants in the learning process, they learn to view mistakes as opportunities for improvement rather than sources of shame. Making mistakes and correcting misconceptions build new connections in our brains (Boaler, 2016). If the brain has the ability to adapt in response to productive struggle, why not incorporate mistakes into the learning process? Creating a classroom culture that studies mistakes and celebrates growth supports all students in developing their mathematical potential.

The explicit teaching of error analysis is a powerful tool to help students learn from mistakes. Error analysis involves examining an incorrectly solved problem and analyzing where mistakes occur. Students work backward to identify where errors were made, explain their reasoning, and then solve the problem correctly (Singh, 2023).

The discussions that arise from error analysis also encourage mathematical discourse. An initial "notice and wonder" activity about a problem can serve as a springboard for students to identify mistakes and what may have contributed to them (National Council of Teachers of Mathematics [NCTM], n.d.b). To effectively implement UDL principles, allow students to express their thinking in multiple ways, such as through discussion, writing, or drawing. Figure 3.2 presents a few other classroom strategies to support students in harnessing error analysis to strengthen their math identities.

When mistakes in the math classroom are viewed as inevitable parts of the learning process rather than something to be feared or avoided, students become more comfortable with taking risks. This type of

Figure 3.2 UDL Toolbox: Conducting Error Analysis

Strategy: My Favorite Mistake

This strategy provides a low-risk environment to help students overcome well-known misconceptions and errors related to the topic being taught.

Present a problem and an incorrect solution to the class or a small group. Ask students to make sense of the problem and solve it their own way. Once they've worked with the problem, ask them to offer suggestions on where the error(s) may have occurred.

Questions to support attending to precision:

- Where did you begin looking for the error(s)? Did you start at the beginning? Did you start at the end?
- Do you think this student understood the problem? Why or why not?
- Did the student use a strategy that was appropriate for this problem?
- Were there any calculation errors that affected this student's solution attempt?

Strategy: Math Detective Cold Case Activity

This activity can be presented digitally or kept in a file folder in the classroom for students to work from when time permits.

Create a set of "cold case" files for the classroom that contain math problems accompanied by incorrect solution attempts. Have students comb through the files and choose mysteries they would like to solve. They may work solo, with a partner, or with a team to find errors in the solution attempts.

Questions to guide students' work:

- When did you first realize something was wrong?
- Do you think the student understood the problem? What evidence led you to this conclusion?
- Do you think there was a calculation error? If so, what evidence can you provide?
- What steps could this student have taken to work more precisely toward a solution?

---

classroom environment increases students' sense of self-efficacy in math and encourages them to believe that they can all be math people!

Increasing Teacher Self-Efficacy

Academic self-efficacy refers to one's beliefs in their own abilities and their attitudes about if and how they can achieve academic success (Hayat et al., 2020). Self-efficacy has been identified as one of the most crucial elements influencing student performance. Students with high levels of self-efficacy are more likely to persevere in challenging tasks. They view mistakes and failures as part of the learning process rather than an indictment of their own abilities. In contrast, students with lower self-efficacy beliefs are more likely to give up on tasks early, postpone completion, or avoid them altogether (Zimmerman, 2000). If bolstering student self-efficacy is crucial to dispelling the Math Person Myth, what about teacher self-efficacy? As it turns out, it's also important.

Similar to student self-efficacy, teacher self-efficacy refers to a teacher's belief in their ability to "successfully accomplish a specific teaching task in a particular context" (Tschannen-Moran et al., 1998, p. 22). Teachers who possess high levels of self-efficacy have been shown to positively influence student achievement, motivation, and behavior (Kelm & McIntosh, 2012). They also hold stronger beliefs that students are capable of positive change and are more likely to persevere in working with students who experience academic challenges (Banks et al., 2013; Gotshall & Stefanou, 2011). Conversely, teachers with lower self-efficacy regarding their instructional abilities are more likely to attribute student failures to the students themselves; these teachers also refer students to special education more frequently than counterparts with higher self-efficacy beliefs (Chu, 2011; Woolfson et al., 2007). Teachers who lack strong belief in their own skills as educators also expect to experience more challenges with certain students, particularly those from economically disadvantaged backgrounds or students who are transient (Tschannen-Moran & Hoy, 2007).

These findings have huge implications, not least of which is that math teachers with math impostor syndrome may inadvertently create another generation of students who buy into the Math Person Myth. How, then, can adults scarred by prior math experiences escape the ghosts of their past?

One way to start is by reflecting on your past encounters with math. Did engaging in mathematical tasks bring about feelings of competence or defeat? Did you feel like part of a learning community, or were you an outsider looking in? Did you actively participate in math tasks, or were you the student avoiding instruction by running to the pencil sharpener or the bathroom? Have you uttered those fateful words "I'm just not a math person"? What is *your* math identity? If your emotional baggage is filled with calculators, protractors, and slide rules, recognize that the time has come to empty that suitcase. As a teacher, you have the power to stop the cycle of undeveloped math potential, but you must begin by believing in yourself.

Mastery experiences—instructional experiences that resulted in success—have been identified as one of the most powerful predictors for positive teacher self-efficacy (Gale et al., 2021). In other words, the more successful you are at math instruction, the better you feel about your own ability to teach it. This sounds a lot like the findings about student self-efficacy, right? Positive experiences yield stronger feelings of competence and increase self-efficacy. Teachers who lack confidence with math must take time to reflect on their practice. In addition to considering where to improve a lesson, think about what went well and how to build on that success. Engaging in high-quality professional development, participating in coaching or mentoring programs, and diving into resources like this book can also increase teacher confidence.

In addition to mastery experiences, teachers may want to seek out what researchers have dubbed *vicarious experiences*, such as observing a highly effective math teacher or working with an educator skilled in universal design. These types of proximal activities can inspire ideas for implementation and increase self-efficacy beliefs (Protheroe, 2008).

If you lack confidence in your math skills, ask for help. It is difficult to create a classroom climate where making mistakes is normalized if you are afraid of failure yourself. Administrative or coaching support, mentoring programs, and high-quality professional development that allows for the practice of effective strategies will encourage you to embrace your new identity as a math person.

Summary

Though commonplace, the declaration "I am not a math person" has significant consequences. Both teacher and student self-efficacy in mathematics directly influence student achievement. The good news is that UDL provides a framework for teaching in an inclusive environment, eliminating the need for the grouping by ability or labeling some students as "strugglers." Students immersed in a culture of high expectations with scaffolded support gain agency over their learning and build positive math identities.

Learners gain a greater sense of competence with math when they are actively involved in the goal-setting process and equipped with a variety of tools and strategies. Teachers can also develop student self-efficacy by positioning mistakes as opportunities for further learning. Educators must also increase their own sense of self-efficacy and competence through mastery and vicarious experiences to overcome math impostor syndrome. Building positive mathematical mindsets supports students and teachers alike in ending the Math Person Myth once and for all.

The Learning Gaps Myth: Planning with Focus and Coherence

How can educators manage to fully address the mathematics curriculum while attending to differences in students' prior knowledge?

In Chapter 3, we discussed how the Math Person Myth is detrimental to positive math identities. Some students who believe they are not "math people" may be basing that belief on weak foundational experiences in math. As any educator knows, students come to school with a wide range of background knowledge, exposure to instruction, and understanding. Although such variability is natural and to be expected, it can present unique challenges in mathematics, where skills build on one another. In response, some teachers are tempted to hyperfocus on "closing the gaps" for students who have not yet mastered grade-level skills. However, an emphasis on addressing student deficits without ensuring access to grade-level curricula will perpetuate gaps rather than close them (National Council of Teachers of Mathematics & NCSM, 2021). Other educators may view variability in student skills as an issue that is out of their control and impossible to target due to the need to cover a broad range of standards and learning expectations, so they rush to cover curriculum content and miss opportunities to fully address critical concepts. These are the two sides to the Learning Gaps Myth—the idea that student skills and knowledge variability is either the primary focus or a condition outside the locus of teachers' control.

In an age where so much is demanded of educators, it can be easy to default to one of these narrow views of math instruction. In this chapter, we will share how to design lessons that balance grade-level instruction with the need for targeted skill development. We will also explore how the intentional design element of UDL can debunk the Learning Gaps Myth by enabling teachers to plan with focus and coherence.

Offshoots of the Learning Gaps Myth

The Prerequisite Skills Myth

This myth assumes that before students can be exposed to grade-level material, they must first be taught all the "prerequisite skills" they are missing from earlier years. Teachers who adopt this approach believe that they must fill in learning gaps before exposing students to what they perceive as more challenging grade-level content. Yet if students are taught below-level content at a pace that does not accelerate learning, they will continue to remain below grade level. Although mathematics is a subject in which skills build on those previously taught and learned, students will never be ready for grade-level content if they must wait for access to that material until they meet some extraneous milestone.

The Covering the Curriculum Myth

Teachers who subscribe to this myth fall prey to the very real pressures of teaching a significant amount of content in a single year. They plow through the calendar in an effort to cover the curriculum, sacrificing depth for breadth and leaving behind students who require additional support. They give attention and validation primarily to the students who arrive at answers quickly; those who struggle to attain proficiency become disengaged as they watch others perform math "successfully." Under this approach, every student receives exposure to the curriculum and some may even master some standards, but many will fail to understand the content at a deeper level.

The All Standards Are Created Equal Myth

Due to the diversity and unique needs of today's students, teachers are bound to come across children with learning gaps, whether from illness, anxiety, school avoidance, disjointed or interrupted schooling, or any number of other factors. In response to being asked to identify and focus on only the key concepts and essential skills for such students, it is tempting to reply, "But *everything* I teach is important!" We don't seek to minimize the importance of curriculum content or encourage the neglect of certain topics, but we also acknowledge that there are simply some standards and lessons that offer greater leverage points than others, especially concepts that are foundational for understanding of later topics. It is critical, then, to identify those essential teachings and meaningfully allocate time to support student understanding.

Planning with focus and coherence helps move away from the polarities of gap filling and curriculum covering. Focus helps identify which topics should be studied more deeply and reduces the temptation to view all content as equally important. Coherence emphasizes the connections between math topics from one grade level to the next. By harnessing the power of focus and coherence, you can design instruction that is both at grade level and targeted at specific skill deficits.

Addressing Gaps and Extending Learning with Coherence

Many educators have bought into the widespread fallacy that before students can learn grade-level content, they must have mastered all prerequisite skills leading up to that point. However, learning is not quite that linear. Efforts to "catch students up" by teaching them missing skills and content from earlier grades create a vicious cycle where learning gaps are widened through lack of access to grade-level material (NCSM, 2020). Designing with coherence helps support both learners who need assistance with prior skills and those who require greater challenge.

Coherence can be thought of as the relatedness of mathematical topics from one grade level to another. These relationships and connections describe the progression of topics across grades (Common Core Standards Writing Team, 2023). When progressions are closely examined within the context of UDL, educators can draw on these connections to design lessons that provide access points for students based on their current knowledge without sacrificing attention to grade-level skills.

Coherence and progression can be illustrated by viewing standards across grade levels and breaking those standards down into sequential parts. Let's take a look at the following 8th grade problem to understand how coherence is important to mathematical understanding.

> An African elephant weighs approximately 6.9×10^3 kilograms, and a bee hummingbird weighs about 1.6×10^{-2} kilograms. How many times heavier is the African elephant than the bee hummingbird?

The following conceptual understandings on which this task is built are addressed by math standards spanning four grade levels (CCSSO, 2010):

- The structure of base 10, including powers of 10, taught in 5th grade (5.NBT.A.2)
- Positive and negative integers, taught in 6th grade (6.NS.C.5)
- Performing operations with positive and negative integers, taught in 7th grade (7.NS.A.1)
- The use of scientific notation to manage extremely large and small quantities, such as when comparing the weight of an African elephant to the bee hummingbird, taught in 8th grade (8.EE.A.3)

Finally, students should be able to use reasoning to recognize that the solution to the task is not 430,000 kilograms but rather that the elephant is 430,000 times heavier than the hummingbird (see Figure 4.1 for the steps for this calculation).

To identify potential misunderstandings or gaps in knowledge, teachers can implement real-time formative assessment, such as a quick write

Figure 4.1 Exponent Work with Elephants and Hummingbirds

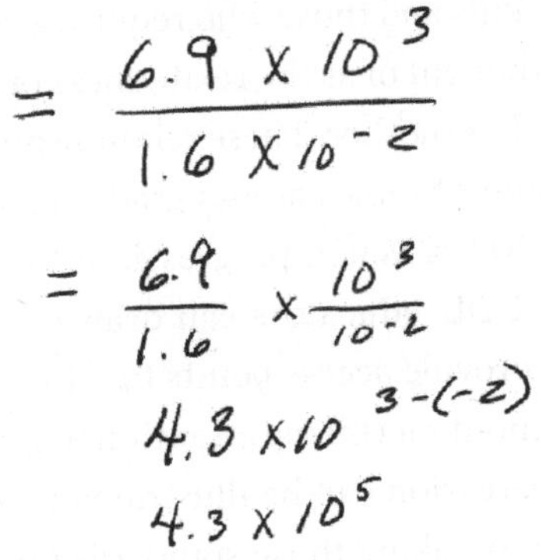

$$= \frac{6.9 \times 10^3}{1.6 \times 10^{-2}}$$

$$= \frac{6.9}{1.6} \times \frac{10^3}{10^{-2}}$$

$$4.3 \times 10^{3-(-2)}$$

$$4.3 \times 10^5$$

with the prompt "Write or draw everything you know about exponents." Identifying standards from prior grades that are integral to performing the task successfully and understanding how they are addressed helps anticipate predictable barriers to learning and allows for proactive planning around those barriers to create accessibility to grade-level work for all students.

Focusing on the Major Standards

Educators who succumb to the myth of covering the curriculum or believe that all standards are created equal may not allocate appropriate time to addressing major standards. Some clusters of mathematical learning demand additional attention and emphasis based on depth of content, time required for mastery, and relationship to future standards and learning (Student Achievement Partners, n.d.). This does not mean abandoning whole segments of the curriculum. Rather, it implies that the amount of time you dedicate to certain concepts and essential skills should reflect their importance. Designing with focus ensures that students will have adequate time to learn the most critical skills in depth, resulting in richer mathematical experiences, discussion, and interaction (Partnership for Assessment of Readiness for College and Careers, 2017).

Clusters of mathematical standards can be identified as "major," "supportive," or "additional" (Student Achievement Partners, n.d.). The major standards are those that require the most amount of time in a given year. Focusing deeply on those standards will provide students with a solid foundation in learning for future skills. Supportive clusters are those that relate to and assist in developing understanding of the major standards, whereas additional standards extend understanding of the major work.

The primacy of the major standards is clear to most educators, but the hierarchy of supportive and additional standards can be more difficult to interpret. Supportive standards can be thought of as those that "set the table" for the major standards. The 2nd grade standard in Figure 4.2 is supportive because it helps lay the foundation for conceptual understanding of multiplication. Although multiplication is not part of the major work of 2nd grade, introduction to the concept of equal groups and repeated addition supports multiplication, which is then addressed in a major standard in 3rd grade.

Additional standards engage students beyond the major work of the grade level. These connections can cross grade levels and even domains. Figure 4.3 illustrates this kind of vertical alignment.

Second graders use models and representations to understand how to add and subtract within the structure of base 10. As they work through this topic conceptually, teachers will want to make connections to partial sums, partial differences, and eventually the traditional algorithms for addition and subtraction. It is worth taking time to unpack this major standard with care and intention so students can begin to work more fluently with base 10 under the 3rd grade standard. The dive into the 3rd grade standard, which is not as deep, builds on the 2nd grade standard.

Figure 4.2 Supportive Standard as Foundation for Major Standard

Supportive Standard, 2nd Grade	Major Standard, 3rd Grade
2.OA.C.4. Use addition to find the total number of objects arranged in rectangular arrays.	3.OA.A.1. Interpret products of whole numbers, e.g., interpret 5 × 7 as the total number of objects in 5 groups of 7 objects each.

Source: CCSSO, 2010.

Figure 4.3 Major Standard Preceding Additional Standard

Major Standard, 2nd Grade	Additional Standard, 3rd Grade
2.NBT.B.7. Add and subtract within 1000, using concrete models or drawings and strategies based on place value, properties of operations, and/or the relationship between addition and subtraction; relate the strategy to a written method. Understand that in adding or subtracting three-digit numbers, one adds or subtracts hundreds and hundreds, tens and tens, ones and ones; and sometimes it is necessary to compose or decompose tens or hundreds.	3.NBT.A.2. Fluently add and subtract within 1000 using strategies and algorithms based on place value, properties of operations, and/or the relationship between addition and subtraction.

Source: CCSSO, 2010.

Some curriculum resources identify the types of standards in each lesson, but unfortunately, we cannot blindly rely on textbooks to tell us what to teach. Equally disappointing is the fact that not all schools or districts have well-articulated curriculum frameworks in place to identify key teachings. The good news is that there are numerous resources available to help us plan with focus. The National Council of Teachers of Mathematics (NCTM, 2006) has identified curriculum focal points that outline the foundational ideas, concepts, skills, and procedures for each grade level. Additionally, many states developed "high-level focus" documents following the COVID-19 pandemic to highlight the major standards of each grade. Internet resources can also be helpful, such as Achieve the Core (https://achievethecore.org), which provides grade-level documents identifying major, supportive, and additional standards and even maps them to frequently used curriculum materials. It is worth spending some time exploring these resources. Figure 4.4 presents a few more strategies to add to your toolbox to support you in planning with focus and coherence.

Clarifying Goals

Units and even individual lessons often incorporate multiple standards. It is important, then, to understand which elements of the lesson are the

Figure 4.4 UDL Toolbox: Planning with Focus and Coherence

Strategy: FastPass Planning

FastPass planning supports students in overcoming barriers related to prerequisite skills they have not yet acquired.

First, identify the major, supportive, and additional standards associated with the unit or lesson. Set the major standards as the focal points for learning and allocate instructional minutes accordingly.

Use coherence mapping to determine previously taught standards and related skills that may create barriers that prevent students from accessing grade-level content. Identify entry points to the content at the current grade level and design learning tasks that build bridges from the prior standards to the standards for the current grade level.

Strategy: Build Bridges to Grade-Level Standards

Smaller, more fluid assessments allow you to bridge a collection of standards from previous grade levels to those in the current grade level. Here are three, smaller assessment activities that can help move your students quickly through their learning.

Quiz Me

Ditch the pages and pages of unit assessments that frustrate students. Build smaller, custom quizzes that reflect the journey students have made from earlier standards to grade-level standards. Target the progression of specific related skills from one grade level to another to make the most of students' precious instructional time.

Interview Me

Create a collection of students' works. Help students organize their work in portfolios or notebooks based on the progression of topics they have been learning. Prompt them or ask questions about their understanding of the skills and standards:

- Show me what you learned about . . .
- What skills or strategies helped you to become stronger while learning . . . ?
- What tools did you use to complete the task? Why did you select that approach?
- What problem-solving approaches were successful or unsuccessful?

Watch Me

Have students work in small groups on tasks along the progression of topics they have been learning. Use formative assessment practices to determine what standards and skills students need to spend additional time on. Ask clarifying questions as students move through their progression of tasks.

---

most critical and focus closely on those areas. Planning with focus and coherence aligns with the UDL principle of "tight on the goal, flexible on the means": We must be clear on the goals of the lesson and know which learning outcomes take highest priority. Then we can offer students multiple ways to access and respond to the content.

One example of the need to clarify and prioritize goals comes from Ms. Highland's 4th grade unit on measurement and data. The goal of an upcoming lesson is "solve real-world problems using area and perimeter formulas." The textbook Ms. Highland uses identifies two learning standards for the lesson:

- *Measurement and Data.* Apply area and perimeter formulas for rectangles to real-world mathematical problems. (supportive standard)
- *Operations and Algebraic Thinking.* Solve multistep word problems involving whole numbers using the four operations and represent problems with an equation using a letter for the unknown quantity. (major standard)

At first glance, Ms. Highland assumes that the main focus of this lesson is area and perimeter. However, upon closer examination, she realizes that "apply area and perimeter formulas" is indicated as a supportive standard. Ms. Highland then rereads the second standard, designated as "major": "Solve multistep word problems involving whole numbers using the four operations and represent problems with an equation using a letter for the unknown quantity." She's not clear yet on how area and perimeter will be utilized to address this major standard, so she keeps reading. The first problem in the textbook reads:

> Eva and Emma are building a rectangular toy box. The area of the toy box is 6 square feet. One side of the toy box measures 3 feet. What is the perimeter of the toy box?

To find the perimeter of the rectangle, students must first recognize that they are missing the measurements of three sides. Ms. Highland now understands how the major standard factors into the lesson—students must find the length of the two parallel missing sides, or "unknown quantity," using their knowledge of area and perimeter.

Recognizing that this is *not* a lesson on finding area and perimeter, Ms. Highland designs her lesson with focus. She understands that the main goal of the lesson is to represent problems with equations, and that the concepts of area and perimeter are used to support that goal in real-world application. Ms. Highland then translates the learning objective into student-friendly terms:

- "I can use my knowledge of area and perimeter to write equations."
- "I can write equations for real-world problems with unknown quantities."

Had Ms. Highland not carefully examined the standards for the lesson, she may have overfocused on calculating area and perimeter and neglected the major standard of representing problems with equations containing unknown variables. Instead, she was able to clarify the goal for herself and communicate it to her students.

Planning Effective Minilessons

An understanding of coherence is needed to meet learning outcomes. In Ms. Highland's 4th grade lesson, she recognized that area and perimeter were conduits for teaching how to write equations with unknown variables. However, students lacking a foundational understanding of these concepts may have a difficult time attaining the objectives of the lesson. Ms. Highland knows that area and perimeter were introduced in 3rd grade and understands that students may need a refresher. She identifies a possible lack of background knowledge on area and perimeter as a predictable barrier for the lesson and plans a minilesson to reintroduce the concepts.

A UDL minilesson is a 10- to 15-minute burst of explicit instruction that contains four components: connection, direct instruction, engagement, and link (Novak, n.d.). The connection component of the lesson focuses on why the topic is important and relevant. Putting this in practice, Ms. Highland asks her students to think back to what they remember about area and perimeter from 3rd grade and share how they might use these concepts in their daily lives.

The second component is direct instruction. This is where Ms. Highland provides explicit teaching on area and perimeter. She posts anchor charts with area and perimeter formulas in the classroom so that students have a visual reference. She also incorporates engagement strategies by having students participate in active learning tasks rather than simply watching her teach. She models an area and perimeter problem and then asks students to complete one with a partner using whiteboards at their desks. This task also serves as formative assessment, allowing Ms. Highland to identify who may be struggling with the concept and who is ready for more challenge.

The final component of the minilesson is linking the learning back to the original goal. Ms. Highland explains that students will apply their knowledge of area and perimeter to writing equations with unknown quantities. She emphasizes the goal of the lesson and directs students to various resources available to support them.

Ms. Highland's minilesson addressed the predictable barrier of forgotten content or lack of background knowledge. Understanding the importance of coherence, Ms. Highland recognized that students might be missing or forgetting some skills that could cause challenges with achieving the learning objectives. To proactively counter those challenges, she explicitly taught the concepts, used formative assessment strategies to identify students who needed more assistance or challenge, and provided resources and visual supports to scaffold learning. Thus, the minilesson set the stage for her to move on to presenting instructional tasks with low floors and high ceilings.

Creating Tasks with Low Floors and High Ceilings

Tasks with low floors and high ceilings (LFHC tasks) can target a wide range of learner variability in classrooms. Tasks with "low floors"—that is, easily accessible and foundational—provide access to all students by identifying skills upon which advanced learning is built. Tasks with "high ceilings" provide enough challenge that even the most advanced learners will experience productive struggle. In other words, "everyone can get started, and everyone can get stuck" (NRICH Team, 2019, para. 2). LFHC tasks allow everyone to find an entry point and everyone to be challenged.

LFHC tasks engage students in deeper exploration of concepts because there is neither a single "right" solution nor a set pathway for completing them. Rather, students use an inquiry approach that reflects multiple solutions and multiple solution pathways. Consider the following task posed to 2nd grade students:

> I wonder how many two-digit numbers have a sum of 9.

Students can approach this task in a variety of ways. Some may begin with their knowledge of single-digit facts. For example, one student may start with 9 + 0 = 9 and recognize that "90" could be one possible solution. Then they might move onto another fact they know, such as 4 + 5 = 9 or 1 + 8 = 9, coming up with the answers "45" and "18." Another student may think more linearly, starting by counting up from the first two-digit number (10) or working backward from the last two-digit number (99) and noting which ones fit the criteria. Still others may use 9-blocks and construct sums of 9 by organizing the blocks in different combinations to identify addends and recording the resulting two-digit numbers. Although the teacher might anticipate that students would employ these solution paths, LFHC tasks leave room for students to develop strategies that they might not have predicted.

An LFHC task like the one described provides an incredible opportunity to incorporate multiple math concepts into students' work. For example, the teacher can reinforce vocabulary such as "digits" and "place value." Algebraic concepts like the identity property of addition and the commutative property of addition can help students to think more strategically and be more efficient in their work. Students can also strengthen their knowledge of single-digit addition facts.

For students who need an extension, the teacher might ask additional questions such as the following:

- I wonder how many two-digit numbers have a sum of 5.
- I wonder why there are fewer two-digit numbers with a sum of 5 than a sum of 9.
- I wonder how many three-digit numbers have a sum of 9.
- I wonder if there will be fewer three-digit numbers with a sum of 5 than a sum of 9. Let's see.

This LFHC task illustrates how to design a task that provides all students with access to an appropriate entry point for a problem. It also shows how to welcome and encourage multiple strategies while connecting to additional mathematical concepts. Finally, it exemplifies the type of task that leaves room for students to grow and extend their thinking coherently.

Summary

Planning with focus involves a deep examination of and emphasis on targeting the major standards, whereas planning with coherence centers on the thoughtful and connected analysis of learning across grade levels. Focus assists educators in clarifying their goals and being intentional about instruction. Coherence helps with developing effective mini-lessons and creating tasks with low floors and high ceilings. Planning with focus and coherence is key to providing mathematics instruction that addresses grade-level content while meeting the needs of students at varying levels of understanding and experience.

Students who have not yet achieved grade-level skills nevertheless can and should be instructed with grade-level content. However, doing so requires rejecting the myth that learning is a lockstep, linear process in which students must master prerequisite skills before being deemed worthy to access grade-level curricula. On the flip side, educators must also disabuse themselves of the notion that every standard is of equal importance and must be addressed in a frenzied rush to cover the curriculum.

Neither side of the Learning Gaps Myth coin is effective in meeting the needs of math learners. By thoughtfully applying focus and coherence to lesson planning, teachers are better equipped to simultaneously target the major standards, address learning gaps, and provide challenge for students who need it. The practice of designing instruction with student variability in mind and anticipating and responding to predictable learning barriers is highly compatible with a UDL approach.

The Answer Getting Myth: Developing Conceptual Understanding

How do we develop conceptual understanding in a way that promotes creativity and productive struggle without overreliance on tips and tricks?

Solving math problems is often couched in binary terms—you either have the answer or you don't. The answer is right or it's wrong. A person is good at math or they're not. But defining mathematics success using such narrow criteria is highly problematic for a number of reasons.

Overemphasizing the end result—prioritizing answer getting—may result in students arriving at correct solutions but lacking the conceptual understanding to explain the work they have just completed. This false sense of proficiency leads to good grades in the present but creates a weak foundation for future mathematics learning. Additionally, students who are unable to answer a problem correctly may become discouraged and eventually begin internalizing the belief that they simply aren't good at math.

The reality is that math is about much more than answer getting. Success in mathematics is about selecting tools and strategies appropriate to the task. It means that students are able to explain their understanding of mathematical concepts and why they work. The processes of problem solving and critical thinking are equally as valuable as arriving at the correct answer.

In this chapter, we will share how to implement universally designed strategies to support a new vision of student success in mathematics. These practices are both inclusive and research-based, and they align with the Standards for Mathematical Practice, or SMPs—processes and proficiencies deemed essential in mathematics education (CCSSO, 2010; see Figure 5.1).

Figure 5.1 Standards for Mathematical Practice (SMPs)

SMP 1: Make sense of problems and persevere in solving them.
SMP 2: Reason abstractly and quantitatively.
SMP 3: Construct viable arguments and critique the reasoning of others.
SMP 4: Model with mathematics.
SMP 5: Use appropriate tools strategically.
SMP 6: Attend to precision.
SMP 7: Look for and make use of structure.
SMP 8: Look for and express regularity in repeated reasoning.

Source: CCSSO, 2010, pp. 6–8.

Offshoots of the Answer Getting Myth

The "Plug and Chug" Myth

This myth assumes that providing students with the proper formulas and tools to arrive at a correct answer automatically results in learning. Teachers encourage students to plug numbers into algorithms and calculators as they steadily chug through worksheets and packets. They may even oversimplify problems by pulling out numbers so students can apply operations without attention to the relationships between concepts. Such an approach may lead to correct answers, but it's also likely to fail at producing understanding of the underlying concept or process. This will likely lead to future misconceptions and inaccuracies, hindering student progression as problems grow more complex.

The Overproceduralizing Myth

Similar to plug and chug, overproceduralizing is the belief that tricks and tips are the best way to help students solve complex problems. These misguided attempts seek to minimize obstacles through catchy acronyms or step-by-step instructions on how to tackle challenging work—strategies that can overwhelm students before they even attempt to solve the problem. Although students benefit from appropriate modeling and explicit instruction, relying too heavily on step-by-step instructions or problem-solving tricks limits the development of critical thinking skills and independent task completion.

The Math Is Boring and Hard Myth

Ask any student who claims not to like math to explain their math aversion, and they will likely tell you one of two things: Math is boring, or math is hard. Where do these beliefs originate? When teachers teach from a single narrow approach and present limited strategies, students who understand the concept find it boring, and those who fail to grasp the content deem it hard. From either vantage point, students view math as a closed process that only values answer getting instead of the engaging and fun subject it has the potential to be.

Conceptual understanding refers to the ability to recognize the underlying principles of a subject (Burns et al., 2015). In mathematics, it can be thought of as a functional grasp of math concepts, a recognition of why a mathematical principle is important, and an understanding of when to apply that concept (Kilpatrick, 2011). When students lack conceptual understanding and merely follow procedures without knowing how and why they work, they are more likely to make errors (NCTM, 2014b). By applying a UDL lens to the implementation of effective mathematics strategies, teachers can counter the Answer Getting Myth and provide access to all students.

Positioning Precision as a Process (SMP 6)

Precision is the ability to calculate solutions with accuracy. Educators under the influence of the "Plug and Chug" and Overproceduralizing Myths are rightly concerned with precision in mathematics—of course they want students to achieve mastery and arrive at correct answers! Yet precision applies to more than just the final answer. Students show precision when they correctly choose and explain their use of operations to solve a problem. They demonstrate precision when identifying and applying units of measurement related to the task. Precision is on display when they compose and decompose numbers using place value and the structure of base 10. Math is made up of multiple different systems and processes, and students with conceptual understanding exhibit precision throughout the use of those schemas rather than only at their endpoints.

A hyperfocus on answer getting negates the importance of conceptual understanding. For an example of how this problem frequently manifests in math classrooms, let's consider Kaitlyn's story. Kaitlyn is a 3rd grader with dyscalculia, a learning disability that causes her to process number-based information less efficiently than those without the disorder. She receives mathematics instruction in the general education setting. Kaitlyn's teacher presented the following problem to the class:

> Mrs. Stanley has 36 photos she wants to place in a photo album. If each page has space for four photos, how many pages will she use?

After reading the problem aloud to the class, the teacher instructed students to solve it independently in their workbooks. She then approached Kaitlyn's desk and said, "Get out your calculator. The numbers are 36 and 4." Kaitlyn retrieved a calculator from her desk, plugged 36 and 4 into the division algorithm, and wrote "9" in her workbook. Kaitlyn's answer was precise, but does she really understand the concept of division?

Consider alternative approaches the teacher could have used. For example, instead of or in addition to providing Kaitlyn with a set of numbers and having her use her calculator to divide them, Kaitlyn could complete the task with manipulatives—blocks to represent photos and pieces of paper as the pages in the album. Kaitlyn could place the blocks on the pages until she arrived at the solution, at which point the teacher could help her make the connection between the work completed with manipulatives and the concept of division as separating numbers into equal groups.

Although activities such as these take time, we must invest in building conceptual understanding before asking students to use algorithms to solve problems with precision. Note that Kaitlyn's use of manipulatives to build conceptual understanding may not always be required. Also note that while this activity is integral to helping Kaitlyn to fully comprehend the content, it would be beneficial for *all* the students in the class. This is a key principle of UDL—what is essential for some is good for all.

Persevering Through Challenging Tasks (SMP 1)

Mathematics problems can often be intimidating and filled with language that creates obstacles for many students. Yet in an attempt to simplify the process, teachers may overproceduralize, especially in the context of word problems. Some teachers use the CUBES method: *c*ircle, *u*nderline, *b*ox, *e*liminate, and *s*olve. Others teach RIDES (*r*ead the problem, *i*dentify information, *d*etermine the operation, *e*vidence, and *s*olution) or STAR (*s*top and read the problem, *t*hink about your plan and strategy, *a*ct/carry out your plan, and *r*eview/check your work). Students are bombarded with these strategies throughout elementary school, often creating more confusion than clarity.

Overproceduralizing problems can also negatively affect students' progress in later grades. Students who rely on procedures without understanding why a strategy is effective or ineffective acquire a shaky foundation for future learning because they lack conceptual understanding. Teachers must remember that experiencing challenge is a natural part of the learning process. Rather than eliminating productive struggle, we must coach students in perseverance and application of problem-solving skills.

Perseverance in problem solving begins by making sense of the task. Students cannot productively struggle through a task unless they can find an entry point with which to start. Examine the following problem:

> There are two restaurants located in the same town. The first restaurant serves 120 customers in one weekend. The second restaurant serves five times more than the first restaurant in one weekend. How many customers are served by both restaurants in one weekend?

This problem contains a lot of language to unpack. Many students will see the word "times" in the problem and quickly multiply the numbers 120 and 5 to get an answer of 600. For these students, there is no evidence that they could not "do the math." However, they neglected to reason through the problem and see that the problem is comparing the number of customers for the two restaurants. Those students also failed to precisely answer the question at the end of the problem. They needed to find out the number of customers served by both restaurants, which involves an extra step. Teachers can address misconceptions by partnering with students to find miscalculations and posing strategic questions to help students make sense of the problem. Figure 5.2 offers strategies to move from overproceduralizing to perseverance.

Developing Reasoning Skills Through Strategy and Tool Selection (SMPs 2, 4, and 5)

What do thinking and reasoning look and sound like in mathematics instruction? Traditionally, math classrooms have often been characterized by memorization and replication. More recent math approaches call for reflection on reasoning. Reasoning requires students to think about real-world quantities and situations and represent them with abstract numerals and symbols. When students reason quantitatively, they are thinking in context of the real world. This is also referred to as contextualizing. Conversely, when students reason abstractly, they

Figure 5.2 UDL Toolbox: Making Sense of and Persevering Through Problems

Strategy: Visual Supports for Verbal Directions

Post common questions that you will pose throughout the problem-solving process, as well as "stop and think" questions for students as they begin self-monitoring.

Starter Questions	Persevering Questions: Stop and Think
• What is the problem about? • What do you notice? • What do you wonder? • Can you restate the problem in your own words? • What do we need to solve?	• What strategy are you using? • What information in the problem helped you to get closer to the solution? • Where did your strategy stop working? • Is there a strategy that might work better? • Is there another way to solve the problem and get the same solution?

Strategy: Response Stations

Create stations for students to visit to respond to questions posed at the onset of a task. Options for response stations may include the following:

- Discussion station—talk about the question with a partner
- Theater station—act out the problem with a classmate
- Drawing station—create a picture or visual representation of the problem
- Model station—build a model using manipulatives
- Writing station—answer the question independently through writing

Strategy: Information Processing

Students may need additional support to organize their thinking around a problem. Use the following tactics to guide students' information processing:

- Embed prompts such as "Does this strategy make sense?" and "Stop and think—does this answer make sense given what I know of the problem?"
- Post visuals around the room demonstrating the strategies that have been taught. Students can refer to these posters until they have internalized the different strategies available to them.

---

decontextualize the problem using a variety of symbols and numerals (O'Connell & SanGiovanni, 2013).

Let's work through a two-step word problem for 2nd graders as a demonstration of the types of reasoning students need to use to find a solution:

> Rafi starts with six toys in his sandbox. He takes two toys out of the sandbox. Rafi's brother starts cleaning up and puts eight more toys in the sandbox. How many toys are in the sandbox now?

In this example, students know that there were six toys in the sandbox, but two toys were taken out. They may begin by reasoning abstractly. They represent this step with the equation below:

$$6 - 2 = 4$$

Now they return to the story, knowing that there are currently four toys in the box. It is important that students return to quantitative reasoning (knowing the number of toys in the box) before beginning the second step of the problem.

Now, with four toys in the sandbox, Rafi's brother adds eight more toys. Students can return to abstract reasoning now that they understand what is quantitatively involved with the second step. Students once more represent the problem with numbers and symbols:

$$4 + 8 = 12$$

To complete their reasoning, students contextualize the problem to understand that 12 toys are in the sandbox at the end of the story.

As adults, we can compartmentalize this thinking very quickly, so it may be hard to remember how we learned to reason through word problems. Therefore, it is quite important that we allow students to migrate between quantitative and abstract reasoning so they can truly show their thinking.

Here comes the warning label. When students rush into abstract thinking without any regard for what is happening in the context of the problem, they can make errors. This is when the pluggers and chuggers need to slow down and reason quantitatively. To aid students in developing abstract and quantitative reasoning, model a limited number of varied strategies that support a given task. We say "limited" because offering too many strategies can be confusing and providing just one way of problem solving is too confining. Model more effective and efficient strategies and allow students to explore their use as tasks become more complex. In addition, give students time to compare and contrast strategies, which enhances procedural skills and fosters the ability to think flexibly to generate multiple solutions (Wong, 2008).

After students have had the opportunity to explore the identified strategies, allow them to use the method that makes the most sense to them. Some students may best demonstrate their knowledge through turning and talking to a partner. For those students, listen as they discover entry points. Others may prefer working independently, writing out the answer or developing a list or chart. Some learners may learn best by creating a model using manipulatives, while still others may prefer acting the problem out or drawing a picture. Encouraging students to choose the method that works best for them not only supports the problem-solving process, it also creates greater equity in math learning by removing barriers.

The introduction of new tools also removes barriers and encourages students to create their own mathematical models. Equations, tables, arrays, number bonds, base 10 blocks, and bar models are helpful tools for representing real-world problems. However, tools are not limited to things students can see and touch. Students will begin to realize that strategy selection and how they apply their knowledge are equally important tools. Even mental math can be framed as a tool (O'Connell & SanGiovanni, 2013).

As you explore equipping students with tools and strategies, keep the following questions at the forefront of your mind:

- Do my students have open access to the tools they need?
- Are the math tasks open enough for students to use a variety of tools to solve them?
- Do I allow my students to reflect on the tools they use, and do I ask them questions about why they used them?

Modeling in mathematics is an opportunity for students to get creative and communicate about math in different ways. It provides glimpses into students' reasoning and how they connect mathematical concepts to the real world. And it dispels the myth that math is boring and permits students to embrace their creativity.

Let's return to the sandbox problem, which Ms. Carroll presents to her 2nd grade students:

> Rafi starts with six toys in his sandbox. He takes two toys out of the sandbox. Rafi's brother starts cleaning up and puts eight more toys in the sandbox. How many toys are in the sandbox now?

Some students in Ms. Carroll's class draw a picture to represent the problem. Others go directly to writing out the equations. However, Nate, who has a learning disability, seems to struggle. Ms. Carroll approaches Nate and asks if there was a tool he could use that would help him solve the problem. Nate requests Unifix cubes (manipulatives consisting of interlocking linking plastic cubes). Ms. Carroll supplies the cubes and encourages Nate to show her what happened in the problem.

Nate explains his reasoning to Ms. Carroll, stating, "The whiteboard is the sandbox, and the cubes are the toys." Nate then places six cubes on the whiteboard. He continues, "Rafi took out two toys," and removes two cubes from the whiteboard. "Then the brother put eight toys away." Nate counts all the cubes and cries, "Twelve!"

Ms. Carroll is excited at Nate's approach to solving the problem. She asks him to tell the story again and suggests that this time they pause at each step and write an equation to match his thinking. Nate is able to successfully produce the work, adding the proper equations without any assistance (see Figure 5.3).

Nate's reasoning was sound and efficient. He met the same expectations as his classroom peers. And because Ms. Carroll empowered him to select a strategy that engaged him in modeling the real-world problem his way, he successfully arrived at the solution.

Figure 5.4 offers a UDL tool and strategies to support students as they develop mathematical reasoning skills.

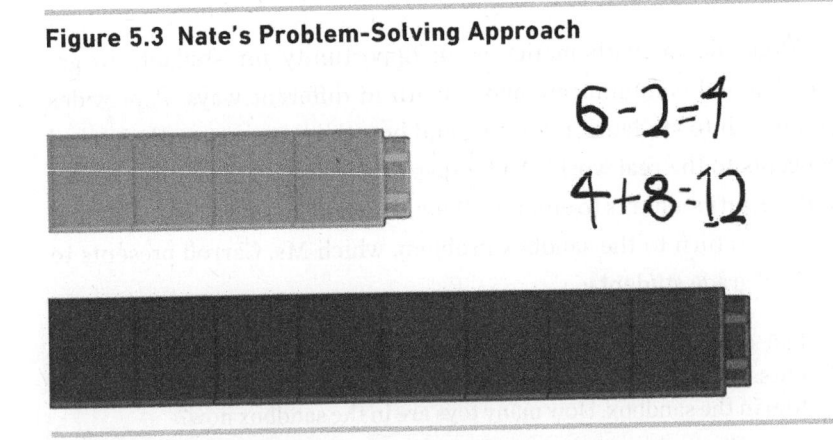

Figure 5.3 Nate's Problem-Solving Approach

$$6-2=4$$
$$4+8=12$$

Figure 5.4 UDL Toolbox: Promoting Reasoning

Tool: T-Chart Graphic Organizer

Some students may respond to a word problem using strategies to represent quantities and situations. Others may find their entry point through reasoning abstractly. To assist students in connecting abstract and quantitative reasoning, have them draw a T-chart. On the left side of the T-chart, students draw pictures, use models, or create informal representations to make sense of what is happening as they solve the problem. On the right side of the T-chart, students represent the problem using numbers, operations, equations, and procedures.

Strategy: Office Hours

Incorporate "office hours" into your daily or weekly teaching practices. As students persevere through solution attempts, they may need your support to reason quantitatively and abstractly. Office hours can provide a safe space for students to reason out loud. While students work independently or at stations, some can choose to enter the "office" individually or as a group. During this time, ask questions that focus on thinking and reasoning. You may also ask about the tools students have chosen to show their thinking. Take care not to give an answer or strategy. Instead, identify how students are reasoning and provide targeted support so they can affirm or adjust their solution pathway.

Strategy: Crowdsourcing

Use crowdsourcing multimedia apps (such as Canva, Flip, or Padlet) to leverage other students as a resource. Students can share their reasoning by posting video, pictures, audio, and text. You and other students can review posts in the classroom community and make connections to others' thinking. Students can also post questions about their reasoning to receive assistance from their teacher and peers. Crowdsourcing creates a safe place for students to solicit and give support.

Exploring Structure, Patterns, and Relationships (SMPs 7 and 8)

Nearly all mathematics is rooted in pattern and structure (Mulligan & Mitchelmore, 2013). Patterns refer to expected regularities in numbers, space, or measures. Structure involves the organization of and relationships between mathematical elements. When students are able to apply their knowledge of pattern and structure, they are better able to reason abstractly and make generalizations (Mulligan et al., 2013). Because an increasing awareness of pattern and structure leads to the development of mathematical thinking, creating opportunities for students to explore these concepts is critical.

You can help students explore pattern and structure in the context of problem-solving strategies. After reviewing multiple strategies with your students, ask, "What's the same about these strategies? What's different?" Once students have uncovered similarities and differences, encourage them to draw conclusions and generate hypotheses about other situations in which the new learning could be applied. They can then test these generalizations to see if they work for other problems.

To scaffold pattern and structure exploration, break patterns into chunks. Let's look at an example of a 6th grade lesson on finding the area of a polygon (see Figure 5.5). Although students may not know a specific formula to find the area of a pentagon in the shape of home plate, you can guide them to think about their understanding of area for other known shapes such as rectangles, squares, and triangles. You might then ask students to divide the shape into known shapes. Then, pose strategic

Figure 5.5 Exploring Structures, Relationships, and Reasoning

Problem

Using the measurements shown in the diagram, find the area of a regulation-sized home plate in square inches.

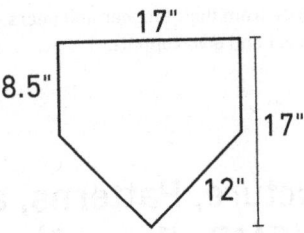

Solution Strategy

Decompose the pentagon into squares and triangles with known measurements to find the total area of home plate in square inches.

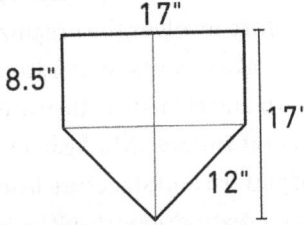

questions to guide learners in determining how to find the area of the original shape by adding up the areas of the known shapes. This reasoning can be tested and repeated by students as they find the areas of other polygons.

Uncovering patterns and structures in math is not just necessary for developing mathematical thinking, it's fun! When we encourage students to "play" with math and explore open-ended tasks, they are able to apply their knowledge using creativity and experimentation. Flexible thinking results in multiple ways for students to approach tasks and discover relationships between concepts. Students who attend to and make use of structure are empowered to extend their reasoning to other problems.

Creating Student Agency (SMP 3)

The ability to uncover patterns and explore similarities and differences in structure also supports students in constructing arguments. Encourage students to discuss both how and why they chose a strategy to arrive at a solution. Although they may have used different strategies, they can justify why they selected those strategies, explain why the strategies did or did not work, and critique various approaches to determine which ones are most effective.

Have open conversations with students about where they are on their problem-solving journeys. When asking students about their work on a task, encourage them to assess their precision. Provide space to openly discuss challenges and possible trends in their mistakes. Put down the proverbial "red pen" and stop slashing through incorrect answers. Instead, view the mathematics classroom as a place to support the development of student agency through problem solving and reasoning.

In a universally designed classroom, students work to become purposeful, motivated, resourceful, knowledgeable, strategic, and goal-directed (CAST, 2017). To develop these qualities in students, mathematics educators must deliver direct instruction in a way that is meaningful, focused, and coherent while also providing students with the space to explore tools and strategies that work best for them in achieving their goals.

Summary

The Standards for Mathematical Practice emphasize the importance of developing conceptual understanding and relationships among topics. Teachers who take a UDL approach to addressing the SMPs recognize that when procedures, tricks, or algorithms are provided prior to conceptual understanding, the learning is short-lived. Mathematical success is about much more than getting an answer. Students exposed to the "Plug and Chug" Myth miss out on the opportunity to discover those relationships and patterns on their own. This robs them of deeper understanding and creates a shaky foundation for learning.

Designing learning tasks that require students to develop arguments, explain their thinking, and critique the work of others helps inspire a culture of curiosity and creativity in math class that sets students up for future success. Teachers can add to this culture of curiosity by providing students with opportunities that support their planning and strategy development.

Finally, when students have opportunities to explore structures, patterns, and reasoning in math, the myth that math is boring and hard begins to melt away. Students are empowered to engage with the content and investigate the relationships they see in the problems. They realize that math can actually be interesting and fun. Incorporating the principles of UDL into the mathematics classroom supports students in attaining conceptual understanding in the ways that are most meaningful to them.

6

The Rigor Myth: Designing Rigorous Learning Experiences for All

How do we provide all students with access to rigorous learning tasks while supporting them in the learning process?

Mistaken approaches to implementing rigorous mathematics instruction can be likened to misguided attempts at improving physical fitness. Some promise themselves, "This will be the year I get in shape" and start by drastically raising the level of rigor in their physical activity. Then, after strapping on their new running shoes, they begin hyperventilating at the end of the block and become convinced that their goal is too challenging or not attainable. Others buy shiny new pieces of equipment, sold on the idea that the device is what they need to produce their desired results. But after an hour of awkward attempts to perform the prescribed exercises, the piece of equipment becomes a very handy, but expensive, drying rack. Still others plot out a plan so slow and methodical that it takes ages for any real improvement to occur.

These approaches generally end with very little success. They often result in frustration, abandonment of the goal, and even contempt for those who somehow are able to meet such goals. Individuals who approach physical fitness as a process, however, tend to find more success. They make shifts in their behavior and mindset. They eat better foods and drink more water. They seek out activities that meet them where they are while setting a path for growth. They are patient, understanding that strength and endurance grow in increments, not through spikes in intensive activity.

So what does this have to do with rigorous math instruction? *Everything!* Teacher perceptions of "rigor" can influence how math instruction is designed and ultimately shape students' math identities. This chapter will introduce a new vision of rigor to counter the myth that rigor can only be achieved through teaching excessively challenging tasks. Instead, we present rigor as a thorough and balanced process that emphasizes the importance of conceptual understanding, procedural fluency, and application. We embrace the ideal that all students can learn math and reject the lowering of standards for certain students.

Offshoots of the Rigor Myth

Rigorous Means Impossibly High Standards

Teachers who buy into this myth believe that rigorous math instruction means designing lessons that are overly challenging. They introduce arduous tasks without properly scaffolding instruction, or feed students a steady diet of algorithms to be practiced incessantly until perfection is achieved. Educators who create overly challenging mathematical tasks absent scaffolding may have good intentions of holding their students to a lofty standard. However, high expectations must be paired with support in meeting those expectations, as well as reflection on one's own practices and ability to reach students.

The "Poor Babies" Myth

In contrast to the "make math really hard" approach, the "poor babies" philosophy is grounded in the well-meaning but misplaced desire to protect students from challenging work. Students with different backgrounds, abilities, cultures, or social identities from the dominant norm of the school or staff are particularly vulnerable to this approach when their teachers equate difference with "less able than." These educators may feel guilty putting students through demanding math tasks, fearful that students will emerge defeated. Rigorous mathematics instruction is deemed "developmentally inappropriate," standards are lowered, and students are shielded from expectations that teachers presume to be unrealistic. This results in what has been coined "the soft bigotry of low expectations"—the notion that certain children have life experiences or characteristics that decrease their chances for success in schools (Bush, 2000).

The Math Entitlement Myth

This myth asserts that only the best of the best, the cream of the crop, the most gifted students are worthy of rigorous instruction. This concept tends to be most prevalent in systems that track and level students or in affluent communities where the majority of students come to school already equipped with a high degree of background knowledge. Families and teachers of students who demonstrate mathematical talent correctly believe that advanced learners are entitled to rigorous mathematics instruction. However, all students are entitled to learn math at high levels. Communities that accept the myth of math entitlement relegate students who need a different presentation or who do not grasp concepts immediately to lower tracks because they "can't keep up" with the pace of this "rigorous" instruction. Such sorting and labeling of students often occurs in the upper elementary grades, setting students on a trajectory of learning that prevents access to higher-level mathematics instruction later in life.

A rigorous classroom is one in which all students receive strong instruction, experience deeply engaging experiences, and take part in grade-appropriate assignments with teachers who support them in achieving at high levels. Teaching with rigor does not over- or underemphasize procedural fluency and conceptual understanding but addresses those constructs in an interrelated way. Rigorous instruction entails modeling the use of flexible thinking, presenting students with opportunities to apply their learning through real-world tasks, and promoting mathematical discourse through intentional design.

Developing Procedural Fluency Alongside Conceptual Understanding

Educators can develop a rigorous mathematics culture by recognizing that mathematics is not a lockstep, linear process. This recognition leads to conceptual understanding and procedural fluency being taught alongside one another rather than as separate tasks. As we discussed in Chapter 4, conceptual understanding refers to the foundational knowledge of a concept, awareness of why that concept is important, and understanding how and when to use it. Procedural fluency is the ability to use mathematical procedures with accuracy, efficiency, and flexibility; understand how to apply the procedures to different contexts; and identify a procedure appropriate to the task (NCTM, 2014b). Conceptual understanding and procedural fluency are symbiotic and overlapping (Powell et al., 2022).

The interdependence of conceptual understanding and procedural fluency can be illustrated through the topic of multiplication. For many years, multiplication was taught as the rote memorization of isolated facts using single digits to be recalled and performed. This overemphasis on procedural fluency frames multiplication with one distinct entry point: memorizing the single-digit times table. But multiplication is much more than that.

To build conceptual understanding of multiplication, students must start with learning the concepts of equal groups, or fair shares. This understanding is then extended to the idea that multiplication is repeated addition. Figure 6.1 depicts three ways to model 3×3 conceptually.

When multiplication is taught only through the memorization of facts, students may not truly comprehend the concept of fair shares

Figure 6.1 Conceptual Models of Multiplication

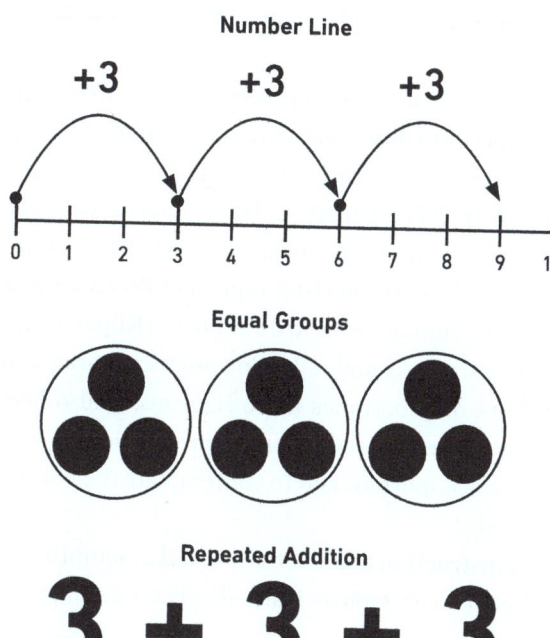

and multiplication as repeated addition. When procedures or facts are taught absent conceptual understanding, students are robbed of opportunities to think and reason. In fact, overpracticing procedures without diving deeper can actually interfere with students' ability to make sense of those procedures (Hiebert, 1999). This creates additional challenges later in learning, when students encounter more complex problems that cannot be solved through relying on memory.

Yet just as procedures should not be taught absent conceptual understanding, the development of conceptual understanding requires exposure to procedures. It is a symbiotic relationship. For example, as you teach students how to find the area of a triangle, you will want to encourage students to discuss the angles that make up the triangle and the various shapes contained within (conceptual understanding). As students explore, you can introduce the formula to calculate area (procedural fluency). In this example, students' conceptual understanding of area is improved through knowledge of the procedure, while procedural knowledge is bolstered by conceptual understanding of why the procedure works.

Figure 6.2 offers some tools for fostering both conceptual understanding and procedural fluency. Using a UDL approach for this process supports a rigorous math experience. The discussion that follows a "brain dump" or model construction builds deeper learning of the utility of different representations in various contexts. Conceptual understanding is enriched by connecting representations with one another and understanding similarities and differences (Kilpatrick, 2011). When conceptual understanding and reflection are incorporated into instruction, learning not only becomes more rigorous, it also becomes more accessible. This is because reflection requires students to deeply consider why a topic is important and to contemplate the best methodology to approach a task.

This type of instruction takes both time and a commitment to seeking connections between previously learned concepts and prescribed skills

---

Figure 6.2 UDL Toolbox: Developing Conceptual Understanding

Strategy: Brain Dump

Ask students to record all the things they currently know about the topic on a piece of paper. They may draw pictures, use text, describe examples, or use any other type of representation to communicate what they know. This exercise makes students' thinking visible. Brain Dumps help you assess whether students already have an understanding of the topic and where their misconceptions may lie.

Brain Dumps serve several purposes. First, they help students move information from their long-term memory to their working memory. They also provide a point of discussion in a low-risk environment before you introduce students to the topic. Students gain an awareness of what they know and what they need to learn. And you can use this information to drive classroom instruction and work with students to create goals.

Tool: Manipulatives and Models

Ask students to demonstrate their understanding of the concept using manipulatives and models. As in the multiplication example, students might begin by constructing models with equal groups and arrays. Next, have students engage in discourse with one another about how their models represent multiplication.

and standards. If you skip conceptual understanding in multiplication and go straight to teaching math facts and procedural skills and fluency, students will never acquire a deeper understanding of math. Ultimately, gaps in conceptual understanding can inhibit students' ability to acquire new information in their current level as well as in grade levels to come.

Improving Fluency While Maintaining Rigor and Access to Grade-Level Instruction

Teachers who believe that rigor means making math overly challenging may be inflexible graders, penalizing students for accuracy errors even when the procedures used to solve the problem are correct. On the other hand, educators who embrace the "Poor Babies" Myth may set shallow expectations for learning, convinced that students cannot move on to more rigorous tasks until they have mastered basic facts. A happy medium must exist. To resolve the tension between these two approaches, we need to understand the difference between math fluency and automaticity.

Procedural fluency is often mistakenly viewed as knowledge of math facts. Fluency refers to the ability to apply mathematical skills and knowledge flexibly, accurately, and efficiently. Automaticity is the ability to arrive at an answer from memory, rather than using calculations (Stickney et al., 2012). Automaticity is a component of fluency. Educators must be careful not to overfocus on automaticity to the exclusion of other facets of fluency.

This can be challenging, especially when knowledge of mathematical facts is embedded within a problem. However, teachers must remain clear on the goal of the lesson. If conceptual understanding of a topic is the goal (as opposed to the mastery of facts), accommodations must be in place for students who are weak in automaticity so that they still have access to grade-level topics. Supportive tools such as number charts, calculators, and manipulatives may be necessary to allow students to participate in the lesson in a meaningful way.

Providing students with access to supportive tools does not mean that automaticity and procedural fluency can be ignored. As previously mentioned, procedural fluency assists with conceptual understanding. Therefore, teachers cannot simply hand students calculators and exempt them from learning their facts. The good news is that effective methods of teaching procedural fluency are highly compatible with UDL strategies that support a diverse range of learners.

When teaching students basic facts, it is important to introduce reasoning and number relationships, not simply rote memorization. Students taught in this way have been found to outperform those who learn from more basic approaches (Baroody et al., 2016; Brendefur et al., 2015; Henry & Brown, 2008). When students are not yet procedurally fluent, teachers must carefully consider how to build fluency skills within the context of grade-level instruction. Traditional methods of whole-group instruction can leave struggling students feeling isolated and disengaged. Providing instruction using a single method limits opportunities for small-group, targeted skill work. Students will benefit from a different approach, such as delivering minilessons followed by opportunities for differentiated tasks based on skill, preference, and tool. Such approaches assist the teacher in allocating time to fostering procedural fluency.

Let's look in on Mrs. Heyl, a 5th grade teacher preparing lessons focusing on teaching her class to use the traditional multiplication algorithm. Students are expected to fluently multiply multidigit numbers using the algorithm. However, Mrs. Heyl is aware that a small number of her students do not know many of their single-digit math facts. This knowledge gap could create a barrier for these students as they try to practice the algorithm fluently and efficiently.

Rather than removing students from the lesson to memorize their facts, Mrs. Heyl takes an inventory of the math facts her students do know. She finds that her students are most secure with single-digit multiplication facts for digits 0–5. With this information, Mrs. Heyl creates equations using only these digits (e.g., 52 × 45 = _____; 53 × 21 = _____; 304 × 25 = _____). Students can use these equations to learn and practice the traditional algorithm with the goal of fluency, even as they continue to acquire facts that are not yet secure. By focusing on math facts students are secure in, Mrs. Heyl helps students overcome barriers and work toward fluency with the traditional algorithm.

Teaching Flexible Thinking

A key component of procedural fluency is flexible thinking, or using multiple representations in problem solving (Digital Promise, n.d.). Math comprises two types of flexible thinking: representational and procedural. Representational flexibility refers to the ability to think about numbers in multiple ways. For example, a student might represent the fraction one-fourth as ¼, 0.25, or a quarter of a shape. Procedural flexibility, on the other hand, is the ability to choose and adapt procedures to solve problems with efficiency and accuracy. A student who demonstrates procedural flexibility may attempt a solution with one approach, recognize the method isn't accurate or efficient, and switch to one more appropriate to the task or suitable to their own learning preference.

Flexible thinking is not natural for everyone, yet it is vital to higher-level math learning. When teachers model different methods of problem solving and ask students to critique the approaches, students learn to think flexibly. Let's consider an example from a 6th grade class.

Mr. Norton presented a problem asking students to calculate the discounted price of a pair of pants. He asked students to share how they arrived at their answer. Figure 6.3 describes the different approaches two students took.

After reviewing the two approaches with the class, Mr. Norton posed the following questions:

- What do you notice about both procedures?
- Are they accurate?
- Can you make connections between the two procedures?
- How might one be more efficient than the other?
- Would these procedures work if the numbers were much larger?
- If you used a calculator to determine the procedure, would you still be able to reason accurately about the solution?
- Would you use a different procedure? Why?

These metacognitive questions open the door for students to explore a variety of ways to solve problems.

Flexible thinking supports rigorous mathematics instruction because students are able to consider different strategies, evaluate their effectiveness, and apply them to future tasks. Rather than relying on

Figure 6.3 Thinking About Thinking, 6th Grade

Problem: A pair of pants is priced at $30.00. You have a coupon for a 20% discount. How much will the pair of pants cost?

Student A	Student B
• First, I have to figure out my discount by multiplying $30.00 by 20%. • I convert 20% into a decimal (0.20). • Then, I multiply $30.00 by 0.20 to find out how much of a discount I will receive. $$\begin{array}{r}30\\ \times\ .2\\ \hline 6.0\end{array}$$ • Now, I subtract that discount of $6.00 from the original price of $30.00. $$30 - 6 = 24$$ • The pair of pants will cost $24.00.	• I know that I can find a 10% discount more easily than a 20% discount, because 10% is the same as dividing a number by 10. • I can find 10% of $30.00 by dividing 30 by 10. $$30 \div 10 = 3$$ • $3.00 is 10% of $30.00. • Since I'm looking for a 20% discount and 20 is 10 doubled, I have to multiply my answer by 2. $$3 \times 2 = 6$$ • The discount is $6.00. I need to subtract $6.00 from $30.00 to find the price of the pants. $$30 - 6 = 24$$ • The pair of pants will cost $24.00

memorization, tips, or tricks, students use reasoning to determine the best way to solve a problem. Designing instruction with UDL principles presents students with multiple pathways to access information and apply their knowledge.

Applying Learning Through Real-World Problem Solving

Application and real-world problem solving are critical components of a rigorous math classroom. The approach to problem solving in math has evolved over time. Previously, students were taught specific skills with the expectation that they would later apply those skills to solving problems (Martinie & Thiele, 2020). Today, however, a rigorous approach to mathematics instruction includes teaching *through* problem solving. In this model, students wrestle with authentic problems, situations, and concepts. These real-world problems allow students the opportunity to construct meaning.

One barrier to students' ability to solve rigorous, real-world mathematics problems is a lack of scaffolding. Teachers can support learners by using an approach called *reality scaffolding,* in which they begin by presenting a standard problem, and then scaffold the problem to several different levels, each more authentic than the next. At each level, students apply their understanding and procedural skills related to the topic. Students may choose the level at which they wish to engage with the problem while still working with the targeted standard. Figure 6.4 presents an example of this strategy being used with a division word problem posed to 3rd graders.

Embracing rigorous problem solving and providing scaffolding for real-world tasks help students begin to make sense of problems. They

---

Figure 6.4 Reality Scaffolding for 3rd Grade Division

Scaffold Level 1: Standard Problem

Nick lost his mother's phone charger for the third time. Nick's mom wants him to pay for a new charger that costs $36, but Nick does not have enough money. His mom says that Nick can pay her $4 a day. How many days will it take for Nick to pay for the charger?

Scaffold Level 2: Provided Choices

Nick lost his mother's phone charger for the third time. Nick's mom wants him to pay for a new charger that costs $36, but Nick does not have enough money. His mom says that Nick can pay her $4 a day, or he can pay her another amount each day. Nick earns $12 per day walking dogs in the neighborhood. He is trying to choose from the following options to pay for the charger:

- Pay $6 per day.
- Pay $9 per day.
- Pay $4 per day.
- Pay $12 per day.

Which option would you choose if you were Nick, and why? How many days will it take Nick to pay for the charger based on your selection?

Scaffold Level 3: Open Choice

Nick lost his mother's phone charger for the third time. Nick's mom wants him to pay for a new charger that costs $36, but Nick does not have enough money. His mom said he can pay her a little bit each day. Nick earns $12 per day walking dogs in the neighborhood.

Make a plan for Nick to pay for the charger. Choose a dollar amount to pay his mom each day, and then determine how many days it will take. Nick must pay his mom the same amount each day. Explain why you would prefer to pay this way.

learn to organize their math and communicate about it clearly. Ultimately, these experiences deepen students' understanding of the mathematical concepts they are learning (Buschman, 2022).

Promoting Mathematical Discourse and Rigor Through Intentional Design

Asking students to reflect on mathematical procedures can be a dynamic springboard to engendering mathematical discourse. Discourse refers to how students show their thinking and make connections. It encompasses the use of mathematical language and how students apply that language to their reasoning (NCTM, 2010).

Discourse enables educators to see and hear how students make sense of problems as they develop arguments and make connections. Structuring intentional conversations can provide a greater understanding of how students reason and where misconceptions may lie. By listening to students' conversations, teachers can gain a glimpse into their thinking that may not otherwise be gleaned from simply looking at answers.

Recognizing that discourse is a critical component of mathematics instruction, math standards, frameworks, and curricula have evolved to place a much greater emphasis on language. For students with print disabilities, multilingual learners, and those who prefer to demonstrate their knowledge nonverbally, language-laden math curriculum presents as a predictable barrier. However, teachers can implement numerous low-effort, high-return strategies to support their students and counter the "Poor Babies" Myth.

Sentence starters can help all students with asking questions and engaging in conversation. This UDL technique assists with sense making, comparing strategies, and reflection. The following examples could be posted in the classroom or provided to students for individual use:

- The strategy that helped me most with this problem was...
- In this problem, I noticed...
- I believe the student's mistake started when...
- I agree with your solution because...
- A total that might be too high for this problem would be...

Students who have difficulty with mathematical discourse may need to know what it looks and sounds like. One way to scaffold the process is to choose two students to demonstrate it for the group. This Fishbowl technique can be used at the beginning of the lesson to model an upcoming discussion with new content or questions. Fishbowls can also be used in the middle of the lesson to redirect nonproductive conversations or to counter collective misconceptions related to content. Instituting a Fishbowl midlesson would require students to stop what they are currently doing and witness another math conversation.

Reading and speaking about math can be a predictable barrier for multilingual learners and students with communication needs. These students may need time and space to observe as well as opportunities to participate. Pairing children with a single thought partner to engage in math talk can be awkward if language barriers are present. In these cases, using triads instead of pairs can be particularly helpful. In triads, students acquiring a new language or those with communication challenges can observe and listen to other students discuss their mathematical strategies (Conroy, 2022). Pictures, hand gestures, tables, and models can also be used to communicate mathematical ideas to peers in triads (Chval & Chávez, 2011). Speaking is just one form of communication; allow students to communicate their math to their peers using multiple forms of media.

To participate in mathematical discourse, students need to develop their understanding of the vocabulary and language associated with a task. Anchor charts, word walls, and math notebooks can help students organize their thinking and utilize math vocabulary.

Anchor charts are homemade posters that can be created before or during lessons. They might include vocabulary words with mathematical examples and pictures or visual representations. After students receive direct instruction on a topic, they can even create charts of their own to reference when discussing their strategies and comparing work. New ideas from students can also be added to the classroom chart during discussions.

Word walls can also be a benefit to classroom discourse during math lessons. Word walls should be active tools for teachers and students during the lesson. Words should be printed large enough to be visible to all students and cycled in and out, depending on the lesson or unit of study. Visual representations and pictures should accompany words on the word wall.

Math does not have to live in a student workbook or packet. Notebooks are a great tool for students to show their thinking and apply their vocabulary knowledge directly to their work. As students solve problems independently and prepare mathematical arguments, they can apply labels to equations, models, and pictures. Students can also refer to their notes as needed to construct arguments for successful discourse.

In addition to visual and audio supports, movement and gestures can support vocabulary understanding. For example, students can use their bodies to create obtuse, acute, and right angles or depict other mathematical representations. You don't need to limit kinesthetic activities to brain breaks or catchy YouTube videos. When you embed motion and movement in your mathematics classroom, students become more engaged in math and develop deeper conceptual understanding.

Figure 6.5 offers additional ways to promote mathematical discourse.

Figure 6.5 UDL Toolbox: Encouraging Discourse

Strategy: Gallery Walk

Use a Gallery Walk at the beginning of a lesson to help students create entry points into problems or at the middle or end of the lesson to provide ways for students to showcase their thinking.

First, have students complete problems using whatever math tools they deem necessary to show their reasoning and attempts at a precise solution. When the work is complete, have them display it on their desks, and then stand up and walk around the room to survey other students' work. They can leave sticky note messages containing questions, feedback, or even reaction emoji.

After students return to their seats and review their peers' feedback, have them revisit and edit their work. They may also incorporate ideas they gathered from their walk.

Tool: Audio and Video Technology

Students who have difficulties communicating can use video, audio, or augmentative communication devices to record their progression through the steps of sense making, attempting to solve, and producing a final solution. Audiovisual products can be recorded and shared with peers using laptops and mobile devices to keep students in the classroom and taking part in classroom discussion.

Teachers who use a variety of approaches in a rigorous and supportive math culture often describe their classrooms as "motivating," "freeing," and "fun." Such teachers reject the myth that excessively challenging tasks are the only way to create rigor. Yet a rigorous culture of learning does not develop overnight. Some students may be reluctant to participate in structures like the ones we've described if they have never had a voice in math class before. Others may be afraid to make a mistake in front of their peers, sending them further into isolation.

It is important to create low-risk environments for students to take chances by setting a positive tone. Share your vision of a rigorous math class with your students, explaining that "rigor" does not mean "hard." Ask students to share their insights.

Cocreating math-related classroom norms with your students can help foster ownership. Consider including the following sample math norms:

- Before you disagree with a peer, ask questions so you can understand their thinking.
- Support others when they make mistakes.
- Mistakes are opportunities for growth.
- Focus discussion on *how* you got to your solution, not just the solution.
- There are many ways to find a solution to the problem. Your way is just one of them.
- Have courage.

If you truly want students to achieve at high levels in mathematics, let them in on this secret: *All* students can engage in rigorous tasks. We encourage you to develop a common understanding and framework for what a rigorous math class looks like with your students (see Figure 6.6 for an example), post it somewhere visible, and revisit it frequently.

Summary

No matter where students are in their math skills progression, they can and should be exposed to rigorous tasks. Students who some may deem

Figure 6.6 Classroom Poster

Our Rigorous Math Class

Understanding 	We can learn about big ideas in math. What does the math look like? What do I already know that can help me?
Skills and Fluency	How can numbers and operations work for me? What strategies can I use? How can I use them efficiently and precisely? What facts can help me work more fluently?
Problem Solving	How can I use my understanding and my skills to solve problems? How can I make sense of problems? How can I persevere in solving them?

as "struggling" deserve to be respected as learners and given access to grade-level curriculum. Watering down expectations inhibits growth. Communicate to your students that you value their ability to learn and expect them to rise to the expectations you set for them.

Yet remember that rigorous learning experiences do not exclude providing support. Too often, rigor is equated with impossibly high standards, or the Math Entitlement Myth prevails, convincing some that only certain students are capable of rigorous learning. Rigor is much more than a challenging curriculum. It is the balanced and thorough pursuit of conceptual understanding, procedural fluency, and real-world problem solving with multiple entry points for students to acquire learning, express their knowledge, and engage with the content.

It's time to breathe a sigh of relief. Take comfort in knowing that you do not need to frustrate students with complicated mathematics in the name of rigor. Rather, a working understanding of rigor and its three elements will allow you to make strategic decisions that inspire students to grow in their understanding of math concepts.

7

The Single Score Myth: Using Balanced Assessment to Guide Instruction

How do we implement a balanced approach where assessment is part of an ongoing process rather than a single event?

When you think about how to assess your students' knowledge of mathematics, you probably picture paper-and-pencil tests. This is unsurprising; most of us have experienced these as the predominant means of assessment in our own educational histories (Lloyd, 2011). Additionally, you may be unsure about how to implement alternative assessment approaches or institute ongoing measures to check for understanding.

The National Council of Teachers of Mathematics has long promoted a vision of assessment that goes beyond end-of-unit tests. Their recommendations involve varying the type of assessments utilized, implementing ongoing formative assessment that measures student knowledge within and between units, and extending assessment within and beyond lessons (NCTM, 2007).

In this chapter, we will debunk common math myths that frame assessment as the ultimate goal of learning. We encourage you to abandon this rigid view of assessment and instead incorporate assessment as an ongoing process embedded in daily tasks. We reject the myth that math understanding can be narrowly measured by a single construct. Rather, we call for responsive assessment using multiple measures within a coherent system of related topics.

Offshoots of the Single Score Myth

Standardized Tests Give Standardized Results

Despite calls for a more balanced assessment approach, norm-referenced, standardized tests are widely used to measure mathematics achievement because they are purportedly objective (Romagnano, 2001). However, as we discussed in Chapter 5, math is about more than just getting answers, so a single score is unlikely to accurately convey what students understand about particular concepts. Two students who achieve the same score on a test are still likely to have different patterns of strengths, weaknesses, and understandings of the topic. To truly measure what a student knows, we must dig deeper into examining methods of problem solving, patterns of errors, and learning misconceptions.

The Gold Star Myth

When we limit assessment to end-of-unit summative measures, test scores are the ultimate goal. Students who score well on these assessments receive actual or metaphorical gold stars celebrating their mastery of the topic. Although students should certainly be commended for their achievements, end-of-unit assessments should not be the only measures of progress. Teachers who embrace this myth neglect the importance of mathematics as a process, which in turn can lead to the pervasive, previously discussed belief that some individuals are "math people" and some aren't.

Formative Assessment Is as Easy as Thumbs Up/Thumbs Down

Many teachers have grasped the inappropriateness of the Gold Star Myth and recognize that assessment should encompass more than summative tests. They acknowledge that formative assessment, or the ongoing monitoring of student understanding, is a critical component of mathematics education. However, an overly simplistic view of formative assessment is problematic. Strategies such as saying, "Give me a thumbs up if you understand and a thumbs down if you don't" still miss the mark. Formative assessment is more than students telling their teachers whether they "get it" or not. Mathematics educators need a more sophisticated approach to collecting data to guide instruction.

In rejecting this myth, educators realize that standardized assessments are only one way to measure student learning. A multitude of formative and summative assessment techniques are necessary to provide balance and ensure students have multiple ways to demonstrate their understanding. Paying attention to processes and assessing students' ability to apply them correctly and efficiently open the door to making math meaningful to students. You should also remember to "assess with a heart," recognizing that your ultimate goal for your students is conceptual learning, not grade acquisition.

Using Multiple Formative Assessment Techniques

Formative assessment is the ongoing process by which teachers gauge student understanding. Effective formative assessments provide teachers with the evidence that shapes the teaching and learning process. They supply "in the moment" data that reveal student understandings, misunderstandings, and misconceptions (Wilkerson, 2022). When we view formative assessment in this way, it is clear that "thumbs up/thumbs down" is woefully inadequate in providing us with the type of data needed to plan instruction.

Similar to the UDL principle of "tight on the goal, flexible on the means," formative assessments can be viewed in a "tight-loose" manner.

This means that the measures used should be tight enough to assess progress toward standards-based academic goals but loose enough to account for student variability. Let's look at an example of tight-loose formative assessment in a 5th grade math classroom.

Ms. Jackson teaches a 5th grade unit on reading and writing decimals up to the thousandths place. After a minilesson, students deconstruct decimal numbers using multiple tools and strategies, such as modeling with base 10 blocks, using place value charts, and writing in expanded form. As students work, Ms. Jackson circulates the room, asking questions to assess their confidence with both the tools and the content.

At the conclusion of class, students complete an exit ticket that poses the question "How many ways can you represent 2.35?" The tickets present the following answers:

- 2 ones + 3 tenths + 5 hundredths
- 2 + 0.3 + 0.05
- 2 ones + 35 hundredths
- $(2 \times 1) + (3 \times 0.10) + (5 \times 0.01)$

This example is anchored to a specific number (2.35), but it shows that students are able to think flexibly as they apply their understanding of decimals and base 10 representation. The information gathered through the exit ticket also supports Ms. Jackson in understanding how her students process and connect with the mathematical concepts involved.

Ms. Jackson might also consider using the Feedback and Forth formative assessment strategy. In Feedback and Forth, the teacher provides constructive feedback on students' reasoning while asking students to provide feedback on strategies the teacher has suggested or other components of the lesson.

Another strategy Ms. Jackson could use on exit tickets is Feed Up. In Feed Up, the teacher provides students with information about what is coming up next in the unit. For example, Ms. Jackson might say, "I wonder how we could represent that number with one more digit," knowing that tomorrow's lesson will focus on decimals to the thousandths place. Feed Up gives students a look at what is to come and encourages them to begin thinking about the task (Fennell et al., 2022).

Open-ended tasks are another method of assessing student understanding. Open-ended activities provide windows into students' thinking as they apply multiple processes. Consider the following example:

> Callie is at a comic book convention. She passes by a booth with three bins of comics. Comics in the first bin are priced at $0.50 apiece. The second bin contains comics for $1.50 each. Comics in the third bin are $2.25 each. Callie has $10.00. She wants to spend all $10.00 on comics without receiving any change. What combination of comics could Callie buy?

There are multiple solutions to the comic book problem. The task requires students to choose appropriate strategies and communicate their findings using accurate information. They cannot merely compute numbers to come up with an answer.

Open-ended mathematical tasks can be created around a number of topics, such as comics, sports, music, social causes, and travel spots; solicit information from students to determine what is meaningful to them. You can then use those stories to better engage students, showing them how math is part of their world.

Figure 7.1 presents a number of other formative assessment strategies you may find useful in your math classroom.

Analyzing Student Progress and Processes

As you move toward incorporating more open-ended tasks in math instruction, determining how to grade students can be a challenge. Rubrics feature agreed-upon scoring criteria to clearly communicate to students what is expected of them (Hess, 2022). When constructed thoughtfully, rubrics provide insight into how students demonstrate their mathematical thinking and show their reasoning. Rubrics are generally categorized into three types: holistic, analytic, and single-point. The purpose of the assessment will determine which type of rubric is best suited to the task.

A holistic rubric assigns an overall score for a task without assessing each component separately (Mertler, 2001). Because holistic rubrics provide a general picture of a student's overall understanding of a task, they are best suited for summative assessment.

Figure 7.1 UDL Toolbox: Formative Assessment Strategies

Strategy: Math Talk
Provide students with a prompt and have them discuss it in small groups. Circulate, listening in on the math talk to uncover both students' understanding and misconceptions. As you move about the room, ask students to share how they are thinking about the task and whether they have the appropriate tools to complete it. Monitor their reasoning by taking anecdotal notes and using checklists.

Strategy: Math Conferences
While the class is engaged in math centers or independent work, meet with students either individually or in pairs. Have them bring samples of their work and ask them to explain their understanding of concepts, procedural work, and problem solving.

Strategy: Video Journaling
Electronic apps can be incredibly helpful in gaining insight into students' thinking, and an added benefit is that students can use them asynchronously. Students can share their responses with others in the class or privately with you. Video journals can be centered around a specific math task, or students can keep a single comprehensive journal to share with you or the class. A video journal can also be updated frequently as a tool for students to show their thinking and reflect on their growth.

Tool: Exit Tickets
Smaller, more frequent assessments can help students and teachers make more informed decisions. Summative chapter and unit tests bring closure to instruction, even though the learning process continues. Exit tickets provide data you can use to be more agile with your instruction, allowing you to pivot or stay the course according to student need.

Strategy: Math Makerspace
Designate an area of the room as a math makerspace, where students can access a variety of mathematical tools. Post a question on a topic you want to formatively assess, and allow students to select the tools to assist them in arriving at their answer. Circulate and take note of both student processes and outcomes.

Tool: Nonpermanent Surfaces
Individual dry erase boards or chalkboards can help students connect and critique ideas. Ask students to share their thinking or solve problems on whiteboards as an alternative to you posing a question to the class and calling on students one at a time. One benefit of nonpermanent surfaces is that mistakes and misconceptions can be wiped away quickly, allowing the group to progress in their abilities.

Strategy: Feedback and Forth
Provide constructive feedback on students' reasoning while asking them to provide feedback on strategies you have suggested to them or other components of the lesson.

Strategy: Feed Up
Provide students with information about what is coming up next and how the topic relates to what they are currently learning. Have students develop a question about the upcoming topic and share it with you or the class.

Analytic rubrics evaluate the subcomponents of a task (Nitko, 2001). The main advantage of using an analytic rubric is that it provides greater insight into a student's pattern of strengths and weaknesses. Teachers can then use this information to better plan for student variability in both understandings and learning preferences. Analytic rubrics also give more specific feedback to students. Keep in mind that students benefit from receiving such feedback at a point in the learning process when they can use that information to improve upon their understanding. In other words, provide students with feedback early enough in a unit that they can do something with it. Analytic rubrics can be time-consuming on the part of the teacher, so consider where your investment of time will be most valuable.

A single-point rubric simply provides information about whether the criterion for proficiency was met. Single-point rubrics can serve as valuable formative assessment tools, particularly when students are engaged in performance-based tasks.

Let's view how the three different types of rubrics could be used to assess kindergarten students' understanding of subtraction. Students are provided with 10 frames as tools to solve the subtraction problem depicted in Figure 7.2.

The task requires students to use the provided 10 frame to show their understanding of subtraction as "taking away." However, it is important to be on the lookout for students arriving at the correct answer of 4 through an incorrect process of adding four circles to the 10 frame. Rubrics should account for this common misconception.

Figure 7.2 Subtraction Problem with 10 Frame

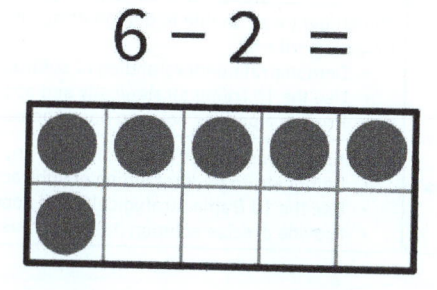

$$6 - 2 =$$

The holistic rubric in Figure 7.3 is summative in nature, assigning students an overall score. This may not be the best rubric for a single task like the kindergarten subtraction example. However, you could use it to summarize a student's proficiency with multiple related tasks assessed with the same criteria.

The analytic rubric in Figure 7.4 breaks the task down into separate criteria. Each criterion is scored separately, allowing the teacher to identify students' comprehension of specific aspects of the task and provide feedback accordingly.

The single-point rubric in Figure 7.5 allows the teacher to assess the kindergarten task quickly. The rubric still breaks the task down into specific criteria but does not specify the depth with which the student meets them. However, this rubric still leaves a lot of latitude for teachers to give students just-right feedback on their performance.

Rubrics are useful for both formative and summative assessments as tools that shed light on how students conceptualize and process information. You can also gather feedback from students about processes that best assist them in learning. Collaborative activities, small-group direct instruction, audiovisual resources, digital software, and independent study are all examples of learning processes that students may benefit from. When we understand how students learn, we can help create goals and processes to optimize their skills.

Figure 7.3 Holistic Rubric

Score	Description
Meets expectations	The student was able to do the following: • Demonstrate understanding of subtraction as takeaway • Use the 10 frame strategically and appropriately • Provide precise solution based on reasoning
Approaching expectations	The student was unable to demonstrate one or more of the following criteria: • Demonstrate understanding of subtraction as takeaway • Use the 10 frame strategically and appropriately • Provide a precise solution based on reasoning
Beginning to work toward expectations	The student was unable to demonstrate any of the following: • Demonstrate understanding of subtraction as takeaway • Use the 10 frame strategically and appropriately • Provide precise solution based on reasoning

The Single Score Myth • 83

Figure 7.4 Analytic Rubric

	Beginning 1	Approaching 2	Meeting 3
Represents subtraction as takeaway	The student was not able to represent subtraction as takeaway.	The student was able to get the correct solution but could not demonstrate understanding of subtraction as takeaway.	The student is able to draw or represent subtraction as items being taken away from a starting number.
Uses tools strategically	The student could not use the 10 frame or any other tools strategically to demonstrate subtraction.	The student was not able to utilize the 10 frame to show take away. However, the student was able to demonstrate understanding using a different tool.	The student crossed out two circles on the 10 frame.
Precise solution is supported with reasoning	The student was not able to determine a precise solution supported with reasoning.	The student has sound reasoning but did not write a precise answer.	The student crossed out two circles on the 10 frame and wrote the number 4 in the equation.

Figure 7.5 Single-Point Rubric

Criterion	Evident	Not Evident
The student demonstrated subtraction as takeaway.		
The student demonstrated addition and subtraction using a 10 frame.		
The student produced a precise solution.		

One way to determine which processes are most effective for students is Four Corners Math, in which the teacher labels each corner of the room with a type of learning process and asks students to move to the corner of the room that is best suited to them. Corner labels will vary by task but may include small-group, teacher-led, independent, video-based, technology-assisted, building-focused, drawing-focused, and so on. Students may choose to work collaboratively or independently. These spaces work best when they are fluid, for example, allowing students to start working independently and then move to a different station to find a different type of support.

Fostering student choice for processes can be quite easy to manage. Consider developing laminated cards or posters with frequently used station or corner labels at the start of the year, rotating the cards out based on the task or lesson. You may also want to use timers and practice routines and procedures for transitions and common activities.

Implementing Summative Assessments

Whereas formative assessments are frequent measures that check for student understanding and guide instruction, summative assessments occur after instruction is complete to provide evidence of and feedback on teaching and learning (Northern Illinois University Center for Innovative Teaching and Learning, 2012). Summative assessments generally have higher stakes than formative assessments, as they evaluate students' learning and often result in the assignment of grades (Yale Poorvu Center for Teaching and Learning, 2023). Therefore, it is critically important that summative assessments align with the goals of instruction for a particular topic.

It is common to see a variety of summative assessment approaches in classes like language arts, social studies, and science. End-of-unit measures in these subjects might include research papers, posters, speeches, or other performance-based tasks. However, these types of summative assessments aren't as common in the math classroom. Just as with other subjects, mathematics students can and should have opportunities to demonstrate their knowledge in authentic and meaningful ways other than the typical paper-and-pencil tests.

An evolving view of assessment suggests that successful mathematics students are able to construct meaning through interpretation and reasoning, in addition to recognizing algorithms and procedures (Mathematical Sciences Education Board, National Research Council [MSEB], 1993). As such, math assessment should encompass more than procedural fluency. Project-based assessments allow students to apply their knowledge of mathematical principles to real-world concepts.

One example of an effective project-based assessment can be found in Ms. Beck's inclusive 4th grade math classroom. Ms. Beck teaches a diverse group of learners, including English language learners and students with a variety of disabilities, some with mobility impairments. At the end of a unit on area and perimeter, Ms. Beck tasks her students with applying their knowledge of area, perimeter, and angles to create an accessible playground. She requires that the playground include certain elements so that she can validly assess students' mastery of all the curricular concepts. This relevant, real-world problem encourages students to think more deeply about the concepts of area and perimeter. For assessment to contribute to learning rather than simply measure it, students must have opportunities to create new knowledge from what they already know (MSEB, 1993). Assessments that mirror learning tasks provide a more sophisticated way to measure student understanding while fostering strategies such as problem solving and critical thinking.

That said, even teachers who craft the most beautiful lessons, implement effective formative assessments, and use multiple measures to assess student learning are generally required to administer standardized summative assessments. With the omnipresence of standards-based reform and mandatory statewide assessments, schools are often criticized for "teaching to the test." Yet as one of our graduate school professors, Thomas Hehir, quipped, "There's nothing wrong with teaching to the test if it's a good test." In other words, if a test is well-designed, reliable, and fair, it can be useful in providing evidence of learning and guide future instruction (Dabell, 2021). Problems occur when students spend the weeks leading up to standardized testing cramming strategies for multiple-choice questions and word problems. Resist the urge to resort to tips and tricks. When we implement intentional UDL mathematics instruction, we equip students with the skills they need to determine the problem-solving strategies most appropriate to test questions.

Assessing with a Heart

Academic assessments are tools that measure students' achievement of learning goals. Teachers who reject the myth that a test score is the ultimate goal recognize that scores and grades are results, not the focus of education. We encourage you to view assessments as useful metrics that inform how close or how far students are from demonstrating skills and understanding. When we approach assessment in this manner, *learning* is the goal. This means that students are provided with opportunities to improve on their work; tests are not "one and done." Instead, students who have not yet attained mastery have chances to remediate their weaknesses and try again.

Some educators reason that providing test retakes or opportunities for revision are unfair to students who perform well on an assessment the first time. Others believe that giving students a chance to revise their work or retake assessments will lead to a lack of effort on initial attempts (Westman, 2018). Such belief systems assume that a single universal construct of motivation exists—that students are motivated by rewards and punishments as reflected by grades (Vatterott, 2015). This mindset positions grades as the ultimate goal.

Instead, we challenge you to set student learning as the ultimate goal. Teachers who provide students with multiple opportunities to achieve mastery realize that a test grade is not the purpose of instruction. Instead, the focus must be on supporting students in acquiring information and demonstrating knowledge of the prescribed standards. We encourage you to reject the Single Score Myth and lead with your heart. Remember that students in your classrooms are kids—kids who make mistakes and deserve opportunities to improve and grow as learners.

Summary

Mathematics assessment is fraught with myths, and it can be hard to break free from these phantom ideals. Yet the National Council of

Teachers of Mathematics (2014b) defines assessment as "a process whose primary purpose is to gather data that support the teaching and learning of mathematics" (p. 89). This outlook on assessment is very different from the belief that its primary purpose is grading and evaluating learning.

Educators who look to a single score on an end-of-unit assessment as a measure of success or failure are playing what Simon Sinek (2020) has referred to as a "finite game." The objective in a finite game is to win. A finite game has a time limit, agreed-upon rules, and a fixed roster of players. Infinite games, however, are different. In infinite games, time runs continuously, rules evolve during play, and the players are always changing. The objective of an infinite game is to stay in the game.

Which game do we, as educators, choose to play?

Educators playing an infinite game design learning around students. They appreciate the fact that there are many ways for students to show their knowledge. Teachers adopting a balanced approach to assessment gather relevant information about their students to assist them in designing instruction while attending to students' variability. They understand that assessment is more than just gold stars and grades—it is a tool to support learning. They measure students' strengths, experiences, and perceptions with a variety of formative assessments to guide instruction. These teachers know that learning does not happen in a vacuum, and they leverage assessment so that they can be flexible and responsive and keep students in the infinite game of math.

8

The All Children, but... Myth: Creating Systems of Equity and Excellence

How can we create systems that promote both equity and excellence in mathematics so that "all" really means all?

"We believe every child can learn."

"Our mission is to prepare all students to become contributing members of a global society."

"All children can achieve at high levels."

Sound familiar? Many school district websites contain variations on the statements above. Yet the districts' actual practices may not always support the slogans espoused in their carefully crafted mission statements.

The reality is that in many places, "all" doesn't actually mean all. When student outcomes can be predicted based upon demographics such as disability, race, gender, socioeconomic status, or another characteristic, the statement "we believe every child can learn," is no more than a hackneyed expression.

Throughout this book, we have shared countless strategies and practices to create equitable and inclusive classroom environments. In this chapter, we will address the systemic and structural shifts necessary to create a schoolwide culture of mathematics achievement that truly encompasses all students.

Offshoots of the All Children, but . . . Myth

The Little Engine That Could Myth

"I think I can, I think I can, I think I can." Most of us have heard of *The Little Engine That Could*, a children's book by Watty Piper. In the story, a little train engine perseveres to conquer a mountain by believing in herself. In recent years, a phenomenon called the growth mindset has exploded in education. According to the theory of growth mindset, individuals can, with effort, improve their ability to be successful (Dweck, 2008). Although it is critically important to foster positive math identities and growth mindsets in students, educators cannot naively believe that these alone are enough. Research on educational outcomes for historically marginalized groups—students with disabilities, Black and Hispanic students, economically disadvantaged students, and English language learners—reveals that these student groups lack access to grade-level, engaging instruction and are subject to lower teacher expectations (TNTP, 2018). Simply encouraging students to change their thinking and attitudes without attending to systemic concerns and instructional practices shifts the "blame" for poor math performance to student attributes and motivation. An overemphasis on growth mindset without addressing the relevance of curriculum, instruction, and assessment ignores the systemic practices that need adjusting (Kohn, 2015).

Excellence Must Be Sacrificed for Equity

A common misconception held by educators and parents alike is that high-performing students will suffer if they are educated in heterogeneous classrooms. Systems that have sought to collapse mathematics tracks have been met with anger and deep concern over the impact on advanced learners (Loveless, 2021). Similarly, parents of neurotypical students have often expressed concern that students with disabilities previously relegated to separate classrooms will negatively affect their own children's learning. Multiple research studies have confirmed that the inclusion of students with disabilities in general education classes has no significant differences for students who are considered neurotypical (Hehir et al., 2016; Kalambouka et al., 2007; Peltier, 2006). Schools that persist in maintaining separate classrooms, programs, and tracks for students perceived as "low achievers" have bought into the false myth that educational equity can only come at the expense of excellence.

Separate Classrooms Benefit Special Populations

The idea that placing students with disabilities in separate, segregated special education classrooms benefits their performance is one of the greatest myths ever told in education. Over 40 years of research has demonstrated a preference for education in the general classroom (Newman et al., 2011). Recent research has confirmed a strong positive relationship between academic outcomes and time spent in general education (Cole et al., 2020). Students with disabilities included in general education have stronger mathematics and reading skills, better attendance, and fewer instances of behavioral challenges and are more likely to complete school than their peers who were not (Hehir et al., 2016). The myth that students with disabilities require separate programming has been debunked by research time and time again, yet the practice is still prevalent. Ignoring this clear, consistent, compelling evidence is an educational injustice to students with disabilities.

We began our careers as public school teachers and then served in a variety of leadership roles—Jenna as an assistant superintendent and special education director, and Ron as a principal and interim curriculum supervisor. We recognize that the privilege of leadership comes with enormous responsibility. This responsibility requires a commitment to advancing both equity and achievement through systemic, structural, and cultural change. Whether you are a former leader in a school or a teacher leader in a classroom, leaders must walk the talk and recognize what "all" really means.

All means all only when a well-articulated math curriculum is available to every student. This occurs by creating intentional structures that strategically apply intervention and enrichment without sacrificing access to grade-level standards. All means all only when separate, segregated special education programs are dismantled, and even students with the most complex needs are viewed as capable and deserving of access to a rich curriculum. All means all when environments, not students, are viewed as problems to be fixed. This chapter is a call to action to create math classrooms where all really means all.

Ensuring Access to a Well-Articulated Math Curriculum

One of the most important systemic considerations for mathematics equity is the provision of a high-quality curriculum. This should be obvious, right? Without a strong curriculum as the foundation, educational outcomes will be uneven. However, many systems take for granted the idea that all students have access to that type of necessary foundation.

A guaranteed and viable curriculum has been identified as the school-level factor with the strongest impact on student achievement (DuFour & Marzano, 2011). Guaranteed means that consistent curriculum content is being taught across courses and grades, and viable indicates that there is sufficient time to teach it. When curriculum content varies from classroom to classroom and school to school within a single system, students' opportunity to learn is highly dependent upon the teacher to whom they are assigned. A guaranteed and viable math curriculum means that learning outcomes are clear, aligned to grade-level standards, and implemented consistently. Materials and resources used to support the curriculum are similarly aligned.

To examine the consistency and quality of grade-level instruction, ask the following questions:

- Is there a clearly articulated, consistent curriculum in place?
- Is the curriculum guaranteed? In other words, if a student moves from one classroom to another in the same grade, would they be taught the same content?

- Is sufficient instructional time dedicated to teaching the standards?
- Is there an overabundance of students referred to intervention?
- Do *all* students have access to grade-level instruction?

If you answered "no" to any of these questions with regard to your school or district, systemic changes are likely necessary. This may mean engaging in a comprehensive curriculum review to identify gaps, redundancies, and inconsistencies. It may require an analysis of schedules and the allocation of instructional minutes. Perhaps it means the district needs to take a close look at the system of interventions and their alignment to the core, or maybe teachers need specific professional development. It might also mean developing a plan for collapsing programs that stratify students based on certain characteristics such as disability.

Students who have not yet attained proficiency are those who are most affected by the lack of a well-articulated, consistent curriculum (Fergus, 2017). Segregating students with disabilities into separate classrooms and tracking students into "challenge" or "honors" math classes at a young age are practices that limit educational opportunities. Students who have been denied access and opportunity require more intervention than adopting a growth mindset.

The assumption that students will be successful if they simply adjust their attitude is troublesome because it attributes poor outcomes in math to student beliefs and mindsets rather than systems that are instructionally or systemically unsound. Of course, building positive mathematical mindsets in students is a component of success, but there are myriad other important factors. Let's face it, while *The Little Engine That Could* is a nice story, the engine wouldn't have gotten over the hill without steam. Similarly, students are not going to achieve proficiency in mathematics simply by believing that they can.

Mathematics policies and practices support equity when all students have access to rigorous pathways (Burdman et al., 2018; Getz et al., 2016). Those pathways must not be based on perception of student skills or arbitrary placement procedures and prerequisites. Equity in math means that students receive both the instruction and the support necessary for success.

Making Strategic Use of Intervention and Enrichment

Once a consistent, well-articulated, aligned curriculum is in place, leaders can work to establish interventions and enrichment services. Notice that we say "services," not "programs" or "classes." Schools must be careful not to replace the core curriculum with interventions for students who need additional supports. Similarly, advanced learners should be presented with opportunities to explore concepts in greater depth and not simply assigned more work or an unrelated special project.

Students identified as having gaps in mathematics knowledge may be placed in intervention programs to address skills they have not yet mastered. Although effective, appropriate interventions that *supplement* the curriculum can be useful, *replacing* grade-level curricula with interventions is highly problematic. This practice maintains student gaps in learning because focusing solely on remediating deficits prevents students being exposed to grade-level content.

The UDL principles identified throughout this book are effective strategies to bolster the quality of core instruction. Once strong instructional practices are in place, schools may consider the use of an intervention and enrichment (IE) block to preserve access to the curriculum while addressing specific student needs (Rufo & Causton, 2022). The IE block is time built into the master schedule to provide support or enrichment. Schools that follow a Multi-Tiered System of Supports likely already have such a block as part of their schedule. Offering targeted, research-based support within the context of an IE block allows students to continue to access grade-level standards with their peers while working on needs and strengths at a separate time.

Incorporating an IE block in a master schedule is an investment of time and resources, so it is important to ensure that the type and quality of instruction occurring during this time is appropriate. When assessing the effectiveness of the IE block, consider the following:

- Is the instruction in the IE block appropriately matched to student needs and strengths?
- If a specific program is being used, is the program being implemented with fidelity, as it was intended to be?

- Are extension and enrichment activities aligned to the curriculum to facilitate deeper understanding?
- What system of progress monitoring is used to evaluate effectiveness?

Dismantling Segregated Special Education Classrooms

"If you build it, they will come." This mantra, popularized by the 1989 movie *Field of Dreams,* holds true for special education classrooms. If you create a separate space for students with disabilities, that's where they will be sent.

We're not going to mince words here. Schools that claim to implement Universal Design for Learning while maintaining separate, segregated special education classrooms have got it wrong. The underlying principle of UDL is inclusion and access. When only some students have access to grade-level math instruction, the goal has not been realized. We encourage you to consider who in your school is included. Do you include everyone, or just the students who are easy to include?

Despite the overwhelming evidence indicating that students with disabilities are best supported in regular classrooms, as of 2021, only 67 percent of students in the United States spend 80 percent or more of the school day in such settings (National Center for Education Statistics [NCES], 2023). It is overwhelmingly clear that dismantling special education classrooms is necessary to attain equity and assist students in reaching their highest potential.

Collapsing special education classrooms in favor of inclusive service delivery models requires a commitment to UDL. Placing students with disabilities in classrooms as they currently exist without a shift in practice will not yield the desired results. Each chapter in this book has laid a blueprint for the shifts that must occur to revolutionize mathematics instruction and provide access and opportunities for all students.

If, as educators, we truly believe that all students can learn and deserve access to a rich and challenging curriculum, we cannot condition that statement with caveats. This means that we cannot leave students with the most significant disabilities and complex needs out of the proverbial equation. Students with complex support needs like intellectual disabilities or autism have historically been removed from grade-level instruction and relegated to mathematical programs that consist of skills like counting change and telling time. Only 19 percent of students with intellectual disabilities are included in general education for the majority of their day (NCES, 2023). We should expect more both from these students and from ourselves.

Using the principles of focus and coherence reviewed in Chapter 4 can help general and special educators identify ways students with significant needs access the major standards. Consider the example of Joey, a 5th grade student with Angelman syndrome who is included in grade-level mathematics instruction. Joey has an intellectual disability and uses a communication device to speak. He requires modifications to the curriculum to access instruction and the services of a paraprofessional, who accompanies him to his general education classes.

Joey's special education teacher supported his participation in 5th grade math by developing modifications in consultation with his general education teacher and paraprofessional. Collaboratively, the team analyzed the major grade-level standards to find entry points for Joey and developed his goals for a place value unit. The modifications are listed in Figure 8.1.

By identifying skills addressed in prior grade levels as well as those Joey will need in the future (coherence), Joey's team focused his curriculum to include access points that were meaningful to him. To assess Joey's understanding of the topic, his special education teacher created a data sheet with each target goal. The sheet included the date the goal was worked on, the learning activity (e.g., ordering objects from greatest to least), and the number of correct versus incorrect attempts. For a summative assessment, rather than requiring Joey to complete a paper-and-pencil assessment that would be very challenging given his physical needs, Joey demonstrated his understanding with performance-based tasks that involved using manipulatives.

Thinking about including students with complex needs can be overwhelming, but there are a number of key points to keep in mind. In an inclusive UDL mathematics classroom, students with complex needs are supported by a team of professionals who collaborate to design

Figure 8.1 Place Value Essential Goals for Student with Complex Needs

Place Value Unit Goals	
Grade-Level Goals	**Essential Goals for Joey**
CCSS.MATH.CONTENT.5.NBT.A.1 Recognize that in a multi-digit number, a digit in one place represents 10 times as much as it represents in the place to its right and 1/10 of what it represents in the place to its left.	Joey will represent a target number (e.g., 0–10) by placing the correct number of blocks on a place value mat. Joey will recognize that (10) 1s blocks are equal to (1) 10s blocks. • When asked to represent the number 10 with 1s blocks, Joey will place (10) 1s blocks on the mat. • When asked to represent the number 10 with 10s blocks, Joey will place (1) 10s block on the mat. • When provided with (10) 1s blocks and (1) 10s block and asked if they are the same or different, Joey will correctly answer "same" given access to multimodal communication (e.g., visuals, device, distal point).
CCSS.MATH.CONTENT.5.NBT.A.2 Explain patterns in the number of zeros of the product when multiplying a number by powers of 10, and explain patterns in the placement of the decimal point when a decimal is multiplied or divided by a power of 10. Use whole-number exponents to denote powers of 10.	Given groups of manipulatives (including base 10 blocks, Unifix cubes, etc.), Joey will be able to sort items from least to greatest AND greatest to least. • Joey will match the number of blocks to the correct number when presented with a number card or asked to respond on his AAC device. • Joey will order a 1s block, a 10s block, and a 100s block in order from least to greatest and greatest to least. Joey will identify the decimal point in a number and identify that a decimal is a part of a number, or less than one whole.
CCSS.MATH.CONTENT.5.NBT.A.3 Read, write, and compare decimals to thousandths.	When provided with two groups of manipulatives, Joey will identify whether one group is greater than, less than, or equal to the second group.

Source: Grade-level goals extracted from CCSSO, 2010.

learning experiences. This is a departure from a system where special education teachers and general educators operate in isolation. The collaborative structures that result from inclusive arrangements lead to elevated learning for all students in the classroom. For example, Joey's general education teacher realized that the manipulatives he worked with to access grade-level content would be useful for all students, so she incorporated them into instruction for the whole class. Finding ways to make content accessible and relevant for students with complex support needs improves teaching and learning for everyone.

Creating a Math Culture That Emphasizes Talent Development

Joey's mathematics instruction was designed around what Joey was able to do, rather than his weaknesses. His team implemented UDL principles to account for his unique learning profile and made instructional accommodations so that he could participate in a meaningful way. Joey was viewed as a capable student, rather than a child whose learning differences required removal and segregation. Under the presumption of competence, his teachers focused on his abilities and held him to high expectations.

Too often, student differences are used to justify exclusionary practices and tracking. For greater equity in mathematics education, we must enact policies and practices that support students in advancing toward their greatest potential, rather than rationing opportunity (Burdman, 2018). Nearly three decades ago, UCLA professor Sandy Astin (1998) spoke of this phenomenon; his words still ring true today:

> We value *being* smart much more than we do *developing* smartness. In our relentless and largely unconscious preoccupation with being smart we forget that our institutions' primary mission *is* to develop students' intellectual capacities, not merely to select and certify those students whose intellectual talents are already well developed by the time they reach us. (p. 22; emphasis in original)

One way to discontinue the practice of valuing existing talent over talent development is to shift how we view challenges. Rather than positioning learning difficulties as problems internal to the student, educators should first look to the system. Across subjects, historically marginalized student groups spend more than 500 hours per school year on assignments that are not aligned to grade-level content (TNTP, 2018). This is equivalent to more than six months of inappropriate instruction. We can and must do better at solving the classroom and systemic problems that are holding students back. Now is the time to stop blaming students and critically examine both instruction and policies.

When we center systemic challenges rather than the student, we focus on what we can control. We can reflect on our teaching, asking ourselves if there is something we could do differently to better reach learners. We can look at the materials and curriculum in place and determine how to make those resources more accessible. Teachers who focus on developing math talent modify instructional delivery before modifying their expectations. These educators critically examine their systems and question inequitable structures that serve as gatekeepers, preventing students from achieving at high levels.

Schedules, pacing, interventions, instructional delivery, and curricular documents and programs all affect learners. To ensure access and opportunity, educators must look through the lens of a designer and interrogate whether and how processes accelerate or impede learning. Are systemic factors affecting instructional time? Are intervention efforts aligned to core instruction, or are they disjointed? Do all students have access to mathematical tools? Are teachers using the latest research-based practices to deliver instruction? Reflecting on such questions is critical to the effort to emphasize talent development over perpetuating existing performance.

Math Myths Busted

Students' mathematical experiences have a dramatic impact on both their likelihood of attaining academic success and their feelings about math. Mathematics classrooms across the United States have been identified as misplacing emphasis on speed, testing, procedures, algorithms, and giftedness rather than problem solving, deeper learning, creativity, and conceptual understanding (Boaler, 2016; Gutiérrez, 2018). These misconceptions are rooted in the math myths that pervade schools.

Now, however, it is time to tell a new story. Designing mathematics instruction with UDL principles can bust these math myths once and for all. Join us in embracing this new narrative:

- We dispel the Math Person Myth, actively engaging learners in building positive math identities, taking agency of their own learning, and viewing mistakes as opportunities for learning.
- We reject the Learning Gaps Myth, using focus and coherence to plan lessons that offer entry points for all students.
- We abandon the Answer Getting Myth, adopting inclusive philosophies that lie at the intersection of UDL and the Standards of Mathematical Practice.
- We rebuke the Rigor Myth and embrace deeper reasoning through conceptual understanding, procedural fluency, and real-world problem solving.
- We dispute the Single Score Myth, recognizing that students can demonstrate their knowledge and understanding in many ways.
- We renounce the All Children, but... Myth, presuming competence in all students and walking the talk by creating systemic and classroom shifts that support historically marginalized learners.

The rejection of these myths lead us to one conclusion: Math is for *everyone!* Math is for students who recite their times tables with automaticity, and for those who still need a calculator. Math is for students who are working above grade level, and for those who have not yet attained mastery of mathematical concepts. It is for students who say, "When will I ever use this in life?" as well as for those who want to be engineers, scientists, or mathematicians. It is for students with disabilities who have previously been relegated to separate classrooms or low expectations, and it is for those identified as academically gifted. An inclusive UDL framework is the antidote to math myths. UDL reduces barriers to learning through intentional design and attention to student variability. By providing students with multiple opportunities to access information, express knowledge, and engage with content, UDL helps educators create a system where we are *all* math people.

References

Aguirre, J., Mayfield-Ingram, K., & Martin, D. B. (2013). *The impact of identity in K–8 mathematics learning and teaching: Rethinking equity-based practices*. The National Council of Teachers of Mathematics.

Allen, K., & Schnell, K. (2016). Developing mathematics identity. *Mathematics Teaching in the Middle School, 21*(7), 398–405.

Anderson, R. (2007). Being a mathematics learner: Four faces of identity. *The Mathematics Educator, 17*(1), 7–14.

Astin, A. W. (1998, Winter). Higher education and civic responsibility. *NSEE Quarterly,* 18–26. https://digitalcommons.unomaha.edu/cgi/viewcontent.cgi?article=1125&context=slcehighered

Bacon, K. (2014, January 14). All along: How a little idea called Universal Design for Learning became a big idea—Elastic enough to fit every kid. *Harvard Ed.* https://www.gse.harvard.edu/news/ed/14/01/all-along

Banks, J., Dunston, Y. L., & Foley, T. E. (2013). Teacher efficacy as a conduit for enhancing attitudes toward teaching reading to African-American students. *Multicultural Perspectives, 15*(1), 19–26. https://doi.org/10.1080/15210960.2013.754286

Baroody, A. J., Purpura, D. J., Eiland, M. D., Reid, E. E., & Paliwal, V. (2016). Does fostering reasoning strategies for relatively difficult basic combinations promote transfer by K–3 students? *Journal of Educational Psychology, 108*(4), 576–591.

Bartlett, M., & Ehrlich, S. (2020, December 16). UDL + design thinking = designing for all learners. *ATD Blog.* Association for Talent Development. https://www.td.org/insights/udl-design-thinking-designing-for-all-learners

Boaler, J. (2016). *Mathematical mindsets: Unleashing students' potential through creative math, inspiring messages and innovative teaching*. Jossey-Bass.

Bolick, K. N., & Rogowsky, B. A. (2016). Ability grouping is on the rise, but should it be? *Journal of Education and Human Development, 5*(2), 40–51. https://jehd.thebrpi.org/journals/jehd/Vol_5_No_2_June_2016/6.pdf

Brendefur, J., Strother, S., Thiede, K., & Appleton, S. (2015). Developing multiplication fact fluency. *Advances in Social Sciences Research Journal, 2*(8), 142–154. https://doi.org/10.14738/assrj.28.1396

Brown v. Board of Education, 347 U.S. 483 (1954).

Burdman, P. (2018). *The mathematics of opportunity: Rethinking the role of math in educational equity*. Just Equations. https://uploads-ssl.webflow.com/61afa2b5ded66610900a0b97/624dd3108c6de38db2c2798a_je-report-r12-web.pdf

Burdman, P., Booth, K., Thorn, C., Bahr, P. R., McNaughtan, J., & Jackson, G. (2018). *Multiple paths forward: Diversifying mathematics as a strategy for college success*. WestEd & Just Equations. https://justequations.org/wp-content/uploads/Multiple-Paths-Forward-Report.pdf

Burns, M. K., Walick, C., Simonson, G. R., Dominguez, L., Harelstad, L., Kincaid, A., & Nelson, G. S. (2015). Using a conceptual understanding and procedural fluency heuristic to target math interventions with students in early elementary. *Learning Disabilities Research & Practice, 30*(2), 52–60. https://doi.org/10.1111/ldrp.12056

Buschman, L. (2022). Teaching problem solving in mathematics. *Mathematics Teacher: Learning and Teaching PK–12, 115*(1), 72–81. https://doi.org/10.5951/mtlt.2021.0255

Bush, G. W. (2000, July 10). *Text: George W. Bush's speech to the NAACP*. WashingtonPost.com. https://www.washingtonpost.com/wp-srv/onpolitics/elections/bushtext071000.htm

CAST. (n.d.). *About universal design for learning*. https://www.cast.org/impact/universal-design-for-learning-udl

CAST. (2017). *Top 5 UDL tips for fostering expert learners*. https://www.cast.org/binaries/content/assets/common/publications/downloads/cast-5-expert-learners-2017.pdf

CAST. (2018a). Checkpoint 5.2. *Universal design for learning guidelines version 2.2*. https://udlguidelines.cast.org/action-expression/expression-communication/construction-composition

CAST. (2018b). *Universal design for learning guidelines version 2.2*. https://udlguidelines.cast.org

Chardin, M., & Novak, K. (2021). *Equity by design: Delivering on the power and promise of UDL*. Corwin Press.

Chu, S.-Y. (2011). Teacher perceptions of their efficacy for special education referral of students from culturally and linguistically diverse backgrounds. *Education, 132*(1), 3–14.

Chval, K. B., & Chávez, Ó. (2011). Designing math lessons for English language learners. *Mathematics Teaching in the Middle School, 17*(5), 261–265. https://doi.org/10.5951/mathteacmiddscho.17.5.0261

Cole, S. M., Murphy, H. R., Frisby, M. B., Grossi, T. A., & Bolte, H. R. (2020). The relationship of special education placement and student academic outcomes. *The Journal of Special Education, 54*(4), 217–227. https://doi.org/10.1177/0022466920925033

Common Core Standards Writing Team. (2023, February 28). *Progressions for the Common Core State Standards for mathematics*. Institute for Mathematics and Education, University of Arizona. https://mathematicalmusings.org/wp-content/uploads/2023/02/Progressions.pdf

Conroy, C. (2022, December 2). *What can a classroom teacher do to make math tasks accessible to multilingual learners?* Presented at NCTM Regional Conference and Exposition, Baltimore.

Dabell, J. (2021, June 23). An introduction to assessment [Blog post]. *Maths No Problem!* https://mathsnoproblem.com/blog/classroom-assessment/introduction-to-assessment

Digital Promise. (n.d.). *Mathematical flexibility.* https://lvp.digitalpromiseglobal.org/content-area/math-pk-2/factors/mathematical-flexibility-math-pk-2/summary

DuFour, R., & Marzano, R. J. (2011). *Leaders of learning: How district, school, and classroom leaders improve student achievement.* Solution Tree Press.

Dweck, C. S. (2008). *Mindset: The new psychology of success.* Ballantine Books.

Elliott, S. N., Kurz, A., Tindal, G., Stevens, J., & Yel, N. (2014). *Mathematics achievement gaps for elementary and secondary students: The influence of opportunity to learn and special education status.* (Research Brief 14). National Center on Assessment and Accountability for Special Education. https://brtprojects.org/wp-content/uploads/2022/05/NCAASE_RsrchBrf14_MathAchievementGapsForElemeSecondStdntsInfluenceOfOTLandSpEdStatus_vFF.pdf

Farrington, C. A. (2013). *Academic mindsets as a critical component of deeper learning* [White paper]. William and Flora Hewlett Foundation. https://www.hewlett.org/wp-content/uploads/2016/08/Academic_Mindsets_as_a_Critical_Component_of_Deeper_Learning_CAMILLE_FARRINGTON_April_20_2013.pdf

Fennell, F., Kobett, B., & Wray, J. (2022, December 1). *Formative assessment: Guiding, informing, and impacting teaching and learning—You've got this.* Presented at NCTM Regional Conference and Exposition, Baltimore.

Fergus, E. A. (2017). *Solving disproportionality and achieving equity: A leader's guide to using data to change hearts and minds.* Corwin.

Ferlazzo, L. (2019, October 19). *Student agency is ownership.* EducationWeek. https://www.edweek.org/teaching-learning/opinion-student-agency-is-ownership/2019/10

Gale, J., Alemdar, M., Cappelli, C., & Morris, D. (2021). A mixed methods study of self-efficacy, the sources of self-efficacy, and teaching experience. *Frontiers in Education, 6*, Article 750599. https://doi.org/10.3389/feduc.2021.750599

Getz, A., Ortiz, H. R., Hartzler, R., & Leahy, F. (2016). *The case for mathematics pathways.* The University of Texas at Austin Charles A. Dana Center. https://dcmathpathways.org/sites/default/files/resources/2016-11/The%20Case%20for%20Mathematics%20Pathways.pdf

Gotshall, C., & Stefanou, C. (2011). The effects of on-going consultation for accommodating students with disabilities on teacher self-efficacy and learned helplessness. *Education, 132*(2), 321–331.

Gutiérrez, R. (2018, February). *Rehumanizing mathematics for classrooms and citizens.* Presented at Critical Issues in Mathematics Education 2018, Berkeley, CA.

Hayat, A. A., Shateri, K., Amini, M., & Shokrpour, N. (2020). Relationships between academic self-efficacy, learning-related emotions, and metacognitive learning strategies with academic performance in medical students: A structural equation model. *BMC Medical Education, 20*, Article 76. https://doi.org/10.1186/s12909-020-01995-9

Hehir, T., Grindal, T., Freeman, B., Lamoreau, R., Borquaye, Y., & Burke, S. (2016). *A summary of the evidence on inclusive education.* Abt Associates. http://files.eric.ed.gov/fulltext/ED596134.pdf

Henry, V., & Brown, R. (2008). First-grade basic facts: An investigation into teaching and learning of an accelerated, high-demand memorization standard. *Journal for Research in Mathematics Education, 39*(2), 153–183.

Hess, K. (2022, October 10). *6 key questions to build better rubrics.* Edutopia. https://www.edutopia.org/article/6-key-questions-build-better-rubrics

Hiebert, J. (1999). Relationships between research and the NCTM standards. *Journal for Research in Mathematics Education, 30*(1), 3–19. https://doi.org/10.2307/749627

Individuals with Disabilities Education Improvement Act of 2004, Pub. L. No. 108-446, 118 Stat. 2647.

Jackson, J., Oberle, S., Haimovitz, K., Shell, A., & Pape, B. (2020). *The Learner Variability Project in the field: A guide to teaching students about learner variability.* Digital Promise. https://digitalpromise.org/wp-content/uploads/2020/09/LVP-Student-Activity-Guide.pdf

Kalambouka, A., Farrell, P., Dyson, A., & Kaplan, I. (2007). The impact of placing pupils with special educational needs in mainstream schools on the achievement of their peers. *Educational Research, 49*(4), 365–382.

Kelm, J. L., & McIntosh, K. (2012). Effects of school-wide positive behavior support on teacher self-efficacy. *Psychology in the Schools, 49*(2), 137–147. https://doi.org/10.1002/pits.20624

Kilpatrick, J. (2011). Slouching toward a national curriculum. *Journal of Mathematics Education at Teachers College, 2*(1), 8–17.

Kohn, A. (2015, August 16). *The "mindset" mindset: What we miss by focusing on kids' attitudes.* https://www.alfiekohn.org/article/mindset/

Küçükalioğlu, T., & Tuluk, G. (2021). The effect of mathematics teachers' self-efficacy and leadership styles on students' mathematical achievement and attitudes. *Athens Journal of Education, 8*(3), 221–238.

Lau v. Nichols, 414 U.S. 563 (1974).

Lloyd, G. M. (2011). The assessment principle: Broadening preservice teachers' views of assessment through engagement with curriculum materials. In G. Lloyd & V. Pitts Bannister (Eds.), *Curriculum-based activities and resources for preservice math teachers* (pp. 69–79). National Council of Teachers of Mathematics.

Loveless, T. (2021, October 4). *Does detracking promote educational equity?* Brookings. https://www.brookings.edu/articles/does-detracking-promote-educational-equity/

Martinie, S., & Thiele, J. (2020, August 18). *The story of problem solving: Looking back and moving forward* [Webinar]. National Council of Teachers of Mathematics. https://www.nctm.org/online-learning/Webinars/Details/485

Mathematical Sciences Education Board, National Research Council. (1993). *Measuring what counts: A conceptual guide for mathematics assessment.* National Academy Press.

Mertler, C. A. (2001). Designing scoring rubrics for your classroom. *Practical Assessment, Research, and Evaluation, 7*, Article 25. https://doi.org/10.7275/gcy8-0w24

Mullaguru, C. (2016, September 27). *Top 5 ways for public schools to better support talented students of color.* Center for American Progress. https://www.americanprogress.org/article/top-5-ways-for-public-schools-to-better-support-talented-students-of-color/

Mulligan, J. T., & Mitchelmore, M. C. (2013). Early awareness of mathematical pattern and structure. In L. D. English & J. T. Mulligan (Eds.), *Reconceptualizing early mathematics learning* (pp. 29–45). Springer.

Mulligan, J. T., Mitchelmore, M. C., English, L. D., & Crevensten, N. (2013). Reconceptualizing early mathematics learning: The fundamental role of pattern and structure. In L. D. English & J. T. Mulligan (Eds.), *Reconceptualizing early mathematics learning* (pp. 47–66). Springer.

National Center for Education Statistics. (2023). *Condition of education*. U.S. Department of Education, Institute of Education Sciences. Retrieved March 27, 2024, from https://nces.ed.gov/programs/coe/indicator/cgg/students-with-disabilities#4

National Council of Teachers of Mathematics. (n.d.a). *Procedural fluency: Reasoning and decision-making, not rote application of procedures position* [Position statement]. https://www.nctm.org/uploadedFiles/Standards_and_Positions/Position_Statements/PROCEDURAL_FLUENCY.pdf

National Council of Teachers of Mathematics. (n.d.b). *What is Notice and Wonder?* https://www.nctm.org/Classroom-Resources/Features/Notice-and-Wonder/Notice-and-Wonder/

National Council of Teachers of Mathematics. (2006). *Curriculum focal points for prekindergarten through grade 8 mathematics: A quest for coherence*. https://www.nctm.org/curriculumfocalpoints/

National Council of Teachers of Mathematics. (2007). *What is formative assessment?* https://www.nctm.org/Research-and-Advocacy/Research-Brief-and-Clips/Clips/Formative_Assessment_Clip/

National Council of Teachers of Mathematics. (2010). *Discourse*. https://www.nctm.org/uploadedFiles/publications/write_review_referee/journals/mtms-call-Discourse.pdf

National Council of Teachers of Mathematics. (2014a). *Principles to actions: Ensuring mathematical success for all*. NCTM.

National Council of Teachers of Mathematics. (2014b, August 11). *Students need procedural fluency in mathematics* [Press release]. https://www.nctm.org/News-and-Calendar/News/NCTM-News-Releases/Students-Need-Procedural-Fluency-in-Mathematics/

National Council of Teachers of Mathematics & NCSM. (2021). *Continuing the journey: Mathematics learning 2021 and beyond*. https://www.nctm.org/uploadedFiles/Research_and_Advocacy/collections/Continuing_the_Journey/NCTM_NCSM_Continuing_the_Journey_Report-Fnl2.pdf

National Governors Association Center for Best Practices, Council of Chief State School Officers. (2010). *Common Core State Standards for mathematics*. https://corestandards.org/wp-content/uploads/2023/09/Math_Standards1.pdf

The Nation's Report Card. (2022). *NAEP report card: Mathematics. National student group scores and score gaps*. Retrieved January 16, 2024, from https://www.nationsreportcard.gov/mathematics/nation/groups/?grade=4

NCSM. (2020). *Closing the opportunity gap: A call for detracking mathematics* [Position paper]. https://www.mathedleadership.org/docs/resources/positionpapers/NCSMPositionPaper19.pdf

Newman, L., Wagner, M., Huang, T., Shaver, D., Knokey, A.-M., Yu, J., Contreras, E., Ferguson, K., Greene, S., Nagle, K., Cameto, R., & Buckley, J. A. (2011). *Secondary school programs and performance of students with disabilities: A special topic report of findings from the National Longitudinal Transition Study-2 (NLTS2). U.S. Department of Education, Institute of Education Sciences, & National Center for Special Education Research. https://ies.ed.gov/ncser/pubs/20123000/pdf/20123000.pdf

Nitko, A. J. (2001). *Educational assessment of students* (3rd ed.). Merrill.

Northern Illinois University Center for Innovative Teaching and Learning. (2012). Formative and summative assessment. In *Instructional guide for university faculty and teaching assistants*. https://www.niu.edu/citl/resources/guides/instructional-guide/formative-and-summative-assessment.shtml

Novak, K. (n.d.). *A teacher's guide to UDL*. Novak Education. https://info.novakeducation.com/udl-teachers-guide

NRICH Team. (2019). *Low threshold high ceiling—An introduction*. University of Cambridge. https://nrich.maths.org/10345

O'Connell, S., & SanGiovanni, J. (2013). *Putting the practices into action: Implementing the Common Core standards for mathematical practice, K–8*. Heinemann.

O'Rourke, M., & Addison, P. (2017). *What is student agency?* EdPartnerships International. https://www.edpartnerships.edu.au/file/387/I/What_is_Student_Agency.pdf

Pape, B. (2018). *Learner variability is the rule, not the exception*. Digital Promise Global. https://digitalpromise.org/wp-content/uploads/2018/06/Learner-Variability-Is-The-Rule.pdf

Partnership for Assessment of Readiness for College and Careers. (2017, November). *PARCC model content frameworks: Mathematics: Grades 3–11, version 5.0*. https://files.eric.ed.gov/fulltext/ED582070.pdf

Peltier, G. L. (2006). The effect of inclusion on non-disabled children: A review of the research. *Contemporary Education, 68*(4), 234–238.

Posey, A. (n.d.). *How to break down barriers to learning with UDL*. Understood. https://www.understood.org/en/articles/how-to-break-down-barriers-to-learning-with-udl

Powell, S. R., Hughes, E. M., & Peltier, C. (2022). *Myths that undermine maths teaching*. Susan McKinnon Foundation, CIS Education Program, & The Centre for Independent Studies. https://www.cis.org.au/wp-content/uploads/2022/08/AP38-Myths-That-Undermine-Maths-Teaching-1.pdf

Protheroe, N. (2008). Teacher efficacy: What is it and does it matter? *Principal, 87*(5), 42–45.

Pruett, S. (2017, May 16). *Exclusive "interview" with the late Ron Mace*. The UD Project. https://universaldesign.org/ron-mace-interview

Romagnano, L. (2001). Implementing the assessment standards: The myth of objectivity in mathematics assessment. *The Mathematics Teacher, 94*(1), 31–37.

Rufo, J. M., & Causton, J. (2022). *Reimagining special education: Using inclusion as a framework to build equity and support all students*. Paul H. Brookes Publishing.

Sinek, S. (2020). *The infinite game*. Portfolio/Penguin.

Singh, S. (2023). *3 tips for guiding students to grow in math with error analysis*. Edutopia. https://www.edutopia.org/article/teaching-error-analysis-math-classes/

Stickney, E. M., Sharp, L. B., & Kenyon, A. S. (2012). Technology-enhanced assessment of math fact automaticity: Patterns of performance for low- and typically achieving students. *Assessment for Effective Intervention, 37*(2), 84–94. https://doi.org/10.1177/1534508411430321

Student Achievement Partners. (n.d.). *Mathematics: Focus by grade level*. https://achievethecore.org/category/774/mathematics-focus-by-grade-level

TNTP. (2018, September 25). *The opportunity myth: What students can show us about how school is letting them down—and how to fix it*. https://tntp.org/wp-content/uploads/2023/02/TNTP_The-Opportunity-Myth_Web.pdf

Tschannen-Moran, M., & Hoy, A. W. (2007). The differential antecedents of self-efficacy beliefs of novice and experienced teachers. *Teaching and Teacher Education, 23*(6), 944–956.

Tschannen-Moran, M., Hoy, A. W., & Hoy, W. K. (1998). Teacher efficacy: Its meaning and measure. *Review of Educational Research, 68*(2), 202–248.

Vatterott, C. (2015). *Rethinking grading: Meaningful assessment for standards-based learning*. ASCD.

Voss, P., Thomas, M. E., Cisneros-Franco, J. M., & de Villers-Sidani, É. (2017). Dynamic brains and the changing rules of neuroplasticity: Implications for learning and recovery. *Frontiers in Psychology, 8*, Article 1657. https://doi.org/10.3389/fpsyg.2017.01657

Westman, L. (2018, March 21). *Retakes do not promote laziness. They exemplify compassion*. EducationWeek. https://www.edweek.org/teaching-learning/opinion-retakes-do-not-promote-laziness-they-exemplify-compassion/2018/03

Wilkerson, T. (2022, June). *Using formative assessments effectively*. National Council of Teachers of Mathematics. https://www.nctm.org/News-and-Calendar/Messages-from-the-President/Archive/Trena-Wilkerson/Using-Formative-Assessment-Effectively/

Wong, A. M. (2008, December 4). Developing flexibility in math problem solving. *Usable Knowledge*. Harvard Graduate School of Education. https://www.gse.harvard.edu/news/uk/08/12/developing-flexibility-math-problem-solving

Woolfson, L., Grant, E., & Campbell, L. (2007). A comparison of special, general and support teachers' controllability and stability attributions for children's difficulties in learning. *Educational Psychology, 27*(2), 295–306. https://doi.org/10.1080/01443410601066826

Yale Poorvu Center for Teaching and Learning. (2023). *Formative and summative assessments*. https://poorvucenter.yale.edu/Formative-Summative-Assessments

Zimmerman, B. J. (2000). Self-efficacy: An essential motive to learn. *Contemporary Educational Psychology, 25*(1), 82–91. https://doi.org/10.1006/ceps.1999.1016

Index

Note: Page references followed by an italicized *f* indicate information contained in figures.

ability grouping, 20–21
abstract reasoning, 52–53
Achieve the Core, 38
agency, student, 25–27, 57
All Children, but . . . Myth
    about, 8–9, 88–89
    curricular quality, 91–92
    excellence *versus* equity, 89–90
    growth mindset, 89
    inclusive education environments, 90–91
    intervention and enrichment, 93–94
    Little Engine That Could Myth, 90
    offshoots of, 89–91
    segregated classrooms, 90–91, 94–97, 96*f*
    talent development, 97–98
analytic rubrics, 81, 83*f*
anchor charts, 71
Answer Getting Myth
    about, 4–5, 7, 45–46, 46*f*
    Math Is Boring and Hard Myth, 47–48
    offshoots of, 46–48
    Overproceduralizing Myth, 47
    pattern, structure, and relationships, 55–57, 56*f*
    perseverance, 49–50, 51*f*
    "Plug and Chug" Myth, 46–47
    precision as a process, 48–49

Answer Getting Myth (*continued*)
    reasoning skills development, 50–54, 54*f*, 55*f*
    student agency, 57
application and real-world problem solving, 68–70, 69*f*
assessment
    about, 75–76
    defined, 87
    formative assessment, 42, 77–79
    Gold Star Myth, 76
    learning *versus* scoring, 86–87
    rubrics, 79–84, 81*f*, 82*f*, 83*f*
    standardized tests, 76
    summative assessments, 84–86
at-risk students, 21
audio technology tools, 72*f*
authors, about the, 2–5
automaticity, 65–66

barriers to learning, reducing, 16–18
beliefs, student, 22–23, 23*f*
Bluebirds and Red Robins Myth, 20
Brain Dump strategy, 64*f*
Brown v. Board of Education (1954), 12
Build Bridges to Grade-Level Standards strategy, 39*f*

Canva app, 55*f*
choice, student, 27, 84
choice boards, math mindset, 23, 23*f*
coherence, 34–36, 36*f*, 41

communication scaffolding, 71
conceptual understanding, 47–48
    and procedural fluency, 62–65, 63f, 64f, 66
connection, 41
contextualizing, 50–52
Covering the Curriculum Myth, 33–34
Crowdsourcing strategy, 55f
CUBES method, 49
curriculum
    covering the, 33–34
    focus points, 38
    high-quality, 91–92

direct instruction, 41
discourse, mathematical, 70–73, 72f
discussion stations, 51f
drawing stations, 51f, 53

educational outcomes, NAEP, 12
educational segregation, 12
end-of-unit assessments, 76
engagement, 41–42
English language learners, 12
enrichment, 93–94
equity and excellence
    about, 88–89
    curricular quality, 91–92
    excellence *versus* equity, 89–90
    growth mindset, 89
    inclusive education environments, 90–91
    intervention and enrichment, 93–94
    segregated classrooms, 90–91, 94–97, 96f
    talent development, 97–98
error analysis, 27–28, 28f
exit tickets tool, 78, 80f

FastPass Planning strategy, 39f
Feed Up strategy, 78, 80f
Feedback and Forth strategy, 78, 80f
Fishbowl, 71
flexible thinking, 67–68, 68f, 78
Flip app, 55f
formative assessment
    minilessons and, 42
    myth of, 77
    techniques for, 77–79

Four Corners Math, 84
fragile learners, 21

Gallery Walk strategy, 72f
goals, developing, 14–15, 15f, 16f, 24–25
    clarifying goals, 38–41
Gold Star Myth, 76
grading, 79–84, 81f, 82f, 83f
graphic organizers, 55f
growth mindset, 89

"high-level focus" documents, 38
holistic rubrics, 79, 82f

"I can" statements, 25
inclusive education, 12, 90–91
Individuals with Disabilities Education Improvement Act (IDEIA), 12
Information Processing strategy, 51f
intentional design, 70–73, 72f
intervention and enrichment, 93–94

kinesthetic scaffolding, 72

labeling and sorting students, 13–14, 20–21
Lau v. Nichols (1974), 12
learner variability, 13–14, 78
Learning Gaps Myth
    about, 6–7, 32–33
    All Standards Are Created Equal Myth, 34, 36–38, 38f, 39f
    clarifying goals, 38–41
    coherence, 34–36, 36f
    Covering the Curriculum Myth, 33–34
    LFHC tasks, 42–44
    minilessons, 41–42
    offshoots of, 33–34
    Prerequisite Skills Myth, 33
learning goals, 24–25
least restrictive environment, 12
LFHC (low floor high ceiling) tasks, 42–44
link, 41, 42
Little Engine That Could Myth, 89
low achievers, 21

Mace, Robert, 11
manipulatives, 53, 54

Martiello, Ron, 4–5
mastery experiences, 30
Math Conferences strategy, 80*f*
Math Detective Cold Case Activity strategy, 28*f*
Math Entitlement Myth, 61–62
math identity
  building positive, 22–23, 23*f*
  Math Person Myth and, 19–20
Math Impostor Myth, 21
math impostor syndrome, 21, 29, 31
Math Is Boring and Hard Myth, 47–48
Math Makerspace strategy, 80*f*
Math Mindset Choice Board strategy, 23, 23*f*
Math Person Myth
  about, 6, 19–20
  Bluebirds and Red Robins Myth, 20–21
  goal setting, 24–25
  Math Impostor Myth, 21
  mindset, 22–23, 23*f*
  mistakes, 27–28, 28*f*
  offshoots of, 20–22
  Struggler Myth, 21
  student agency, 25–27
  teacher self-efficacy, 21–22, 28–30
Math Talk strategy, 80*f*
mathematical discourse, 70–73, 72*f*
memorization, rote, 66
metacognitive questions, 67
microgoals, 24–25
mindset, 22–23, 23*f*, 89
minilessons, 41–42, 66
mistakes, as opportunities, 27–28, 28*f*, 57
model stations, 51*f*
modeling, 53
movement and gesture, as scaffolding, 72
My Favorite Mistake strategy, 28*f*

nonpermanent surfaces tool, 80*f*
notebooks, 72
"notice and wonder" activities, 27–28

Office Hours strategy, 55*f*
open-ended tasks, 79
output, student
  choice and variety in, 18
Overproceduralizing Myth, 47

Padlet app, 55*f*
patterns, 55–57, 56*f*
perceptions, student, 22–23, 23*f*
perseverance, 49–50, 51*f*
"Plug and Chug" Myth, 46–47
"Poor Babies" Myth, 61
precision, as a process, 48–49, 57
Prerequisite Skills Myth, 33
problem solving
  application and real-world, 68–70, 69*f*
  flexible thinking in, 67–68, 68*f*
  perseverance in, 49–50, 51*f*
procedural flexibility, 67–68, 68*f*
procedural fluency and conceptual understanding, 62–65, 63*f*, 64*f*, 85
procedural fluency and rigor, 65–66
professional development, 30
progression, coherence and, 35–36, 36*f*

quantitative reasoning, 52

reality scaffolding, 69–70, 69*f*
reasoning skills development, 50–54, 54*f*, 55*f*
relationships, 55–57, 56*f*
representational flexibility, 67–68, 68*f*
Response Stations strategy, 51*f*
RIDES method, 49
Rigor Myth
  about, 7–8, 59–60, 73–74, 74*f*
  application and real-world problem solving, 68–70, 69*f*
  flexible thinking and, 67–68, 68*f*
  impossibly high standards, 60
  Math Entitlement Myth, 61–62
  offshoots of, 60–62
  "Poor Babies" Myth, 61
  procedural fluency and, 65–66
  procedural fluency and conceptual understanding, 62–65, 63*f*, 64*f*
  promoting mathematical discourse through intentional design, 70–73, 72*f*
rubrics, 79–84, 81*f*, 82*f*, 83*f*
Rufo, Jenna Mancini, 2–4

scaffolding, 25, 69–70, 69*f*, 71
segregated classrooms, 90–91, 94–97, 96*f*

self-efficacy
    of teachers, 21–22, 28–30
single-point rubrics, 81, 83*f*
Single Score Myth
    about, 8, 75–76
    formative assessment, 77–79
    Gold Star Myth, 76
    learning as goal, 86–87
    offshoots of, 76–77
    rubrics, 79–84, 81*f*, 82*f*, 83*f*
    standardized tests, 76
    summative assessments, 84–86
standardized tests, 76
standards, major, 34, 36–38, 38*f*, 39*f*
standards, myths about, 60
standards, supportive, 37, 38*f*
Standards for Mathematical Practice (SMPs), 46*f*
STAR method, 49
structures, 55–57, 56*f*
Struggler Myth, 21
student agency, 25–27, 57, 84
student-centered learning, 26
student choice, 27, 84
summative assessments, 84–86

T-chart graphic organizer tool, 55*f*
talent development, 97–98
teachers
    administrative or coaching support for, 30
    self-efficacy of, 21–22, 28–30
theater stations, 51*f*
thumbs up/thumbs down, 77
triads for communication scaffolding, 71

Universal Design for Learning (UDL)
    about, 11
    defined, 11
    inclusive education, 12
    intentional design of, 14–16, 15*f*, 16*f*
    key components, 11
    learner variability, 13–14
    reducing barriers to learning, 16–18

Universal Design for Learning (UDL) strategies
    Brain Dump, 64*f*
    Build Bridges to Grade-Level Standards, 39*f*
    Crowdsourcing, 55*f*
    FastPass Planning, 39*f*
    Feed Up, 78, 80*f*
    Feedback and Forth, 78, 80*f*
    Gallery Walk, 72*f*
    Information Processing, 51*f*
    Math Conferences, 80*f*
    Math Detective Cold Case Activity, 28*f*
    Math Makerspace, 80*f*
    Math Mindset Choice Board, 23*f*
    Math Talk, 80*f*
    My Favorite Mistake, 28*f*
    Office Hours, 55*f*
    Response Stations, 51*f*
    Video Journaling, 80*ff*
    Visual Supports for Verbal Directions, 51*f*
Universal Design for Learning (UDL) tools
    audio technology, 72*f*
    exit tickets, 80*f*
    manipulatives and models, 64*f*
    nonpermanent surfaces, 80*f*
    T-chart graphic organizer, 55*f*
    video technology, 72*f*

variability, learner, 13–14, 78
verbal directions with visual supports, 51*f*
vicarious experiences, 30
Video Journaling strategy, 80*f*
video technology tools, 72*f*
Visual Supports for Verbal Directions strategy, 51*f*

whole-group instruction, 10, 66
word walls, 71–72
writing stations, 51*f*

About the Authors

Jenna Mancini Rufo is an inclusive education consultant and the founder and CEO of EmpowerED School Solutions. Jenna has worked with state departments of education, disability rights organizations, and school systems across the United States and in Australia to create more equitable and inclusive special education programs. She spent nearly 20 years in public education as an assistant superintendent, special education director, and teacher, where she advocated for students with disabilities to receive services in inclusive settings. Jenna has co-authored *Reimagining Special Education: Using Inclusion as a Framework to Build Equity and Support All Students* and *The Way to Inclusion: How Leaders Create Schools Where Every Student Belongs*. Her professional experiences, coupled with graduate work completed at Harvard University, have provided her with an understanding of both theory and practical implementation of inclusive practices. You can learn more about Jenna by visiting her website at www.empoweredschool.org or find her on social media @JennaMRufo.

Ron Martiello currently serves as a learning coach in the North Penn School District in Montgomery County, PA, and is celebrating his 27th year as an educator. He has served as a 1st grade teacher, an elementary assistant principal, and elementary principal. In 2015, Ron returned to the classroom, allowing him to spend more time with his family. In his 3rd grade classroom, Ron took the opportunity to reinvent himself and hone his teaching practices. He embraced social media and connected with authors and educators from across the country. In 2018, Ron was asked to serve as a learning coach to support teachers in the areas of technology and math. During this experience, he began to dive deeply into the complexities of math learning and instruction. You can learn more about Ron by following him on social media @RonMartiello.

Related ASCD Resources: Instructional Strategies and Equity

At the time of publication, the following resources were available (ASCD stock numbers in parentheses):

Building a Math-Positive Culture: How to Support Great Math Teaching in Your School (ASCD Arias) by Cathy L. Seeley (#SF116068)

Leading an Inclusive School: Access and Success for All Students by Richard A. Villa and Jacqueline S. Thousand (#116022)

Making Sense of Math: How to Help Every Student Become a Mathematical Thinker and Problem Solver (ASCD Arias) by Cathy L. Seeley (#SF116067)

Math Fact Fluency: 60+ Games and Assessment Tools to Support Learning and Retention by Jennifer Bay-Williams and Gina Kling (#118014)

Rigor by Design, Not Chance: Deeper Thinking Through Actionable Instruction and Assessment by Karin Hess (#122036)

The School Leader's Guide to Building and Sustaining Math Success by Marian Small and Doug Duff (#118039)

Teaching Students to Communicate Mathematically by Laney Sammons (#118005)

The Way to Inclusion: How Leaders Create Schools Where Every Student Belongs by Julie Causton, Kate MacLeod, Kristie Pretti-Frontczak, Jenna Mancini Rufo, and Paul Gordon (#123001)

Your Students, My Students, Our Students: Rethinking Equitable and Inclusive Classrooms by Lee Ann Jung, Nancy Frey, Douglas Fisher, and Julie Kroener (#119019)

For up-to-date information about ASCD resources, go to www.ascd.org. You can search the complete archives of *Educational Leadership* at www.ascd.org/el. To contact us, send an email to member@ascd.org or call 1-800-933-2723 or 703-578-9600.

WHOLE CHILD
TENETS

1 HEALTHY
Each student enters school healthy and learns about and practices a healthy lifestyle.

2 SAFE
Each student learns in an environment that is physically and emotionally **safe** for students and adults.

3 ENGAGED
Each student is actively **engaged** in learning and is connected to the school and broader community.

4 SUPPORTED
Each student has access to personalized learning and is **supported** by qualified, caring adults.

5 CHALLENGED
Each student is **challenged** academically and prepared for success in college or further study and for employment and participation in a global environment.

ascd whole child

The ASCD Whole Child approach is an effort to transition from a focus on narrowly defined academic achievement to one that promotes the long-term development and success of all children. Through this approach, ASCD supports educators, families, community members, and policymakers as they move from a vision about educating the whole child to sustainable, collaborative actions.

Conquering Math Myths with Universal Design relates to the **engaged**, **supported**, and **challenged** tenets. *For more about the ASCD Whole Child approach, visit* **www.ascd.org/wholechild.**

Become an ASCD member today!
Go to www.ascd.org/joinascd
or call toll-free: 800-933-ASCD (2723)

DON'T MISS A SINGLE ISSUE OF ASCD'S AWARD-WINNING MAGAZINE.

ascd educational leadership

If you belong to a Professional Learning Community, you may be looking for a way to get your fellow educators' minds around a complex topic. Why not delve into a relevant theme issue of *Educational Leadership*, the journal written by educators for educators?

Subscribe now, or purchase back issues of ASCD's flagship publication at **www.ascd.org/el**. Discounts on bulk purchases are available.

To see more details about these and other popular issues of *Educational Leadership*, visit **www.ascd.org/el/all**.

2800 Shirlington Road
Suite 1001
Arlington, VA 22206 USA

www.ascd.org/learnmore